Jean Epstein

The Intelligence of a Machine

Translated by
Christophe Wall-Romana

L'intelligence d'une machine
- © Independencia editions -

Translated from French by Christophe Wall-Romana
as *The Intelligence of a Machine*

First Edition
Minneapolis © 2014, Univocal Publishing

Published by Univocal
123 North 3rd Street, #202
Minneapolis, MN 55401
www.univocalpublishing.com

Thanks to La Cinémathèque Française,
Jonathan Thomas, Grace Kavanah,
Dylan Hester, and Jon Thrower.

Designed & Printed by Jason Wagner
Distributed by the University of Minnesota Press

ISBN 9781937561185
Library of Congress Control Number 2014930841

Table of Contents

Translator's Introduction:
The Philosophy of Cinema

Jean Epstein (1897-1953) was a noted French avant-garde filmmaker, poet, fiction writer, and arguably the most important French theoretician of cinema before André Bazin. He was born in Warsaw of a Polish Jewish father and a gentile French mother, and his younger sister, Marie Epstein, became his lifelong collaborator and companion, as well as a noted filmmaker herself. Schooled in Switzerland, and already an ardent cinephile in his teens, he moved to Lyon in 1916 to pursue medical studies. He soon began writing poetry, some of which was explicitly homoerotic—Epstein was gay—and from 1920-21 he edited a literary journal titled *Le Promenoir*, and published a series of essays on literature in *L'Esprit nouveau*, a vital journal for international modernism. Around 1918, he became the translator and secretary to Auguste Lumière who, 30 years earlier (1894-95), had developed the *Cinématographe* with his brother Louis—though Auguste was by then weary of fiction films. In 1921, Epstein met the poet Blaise Cendrars who was among the most cinephilic French writers at the time. Through Cendrars, Epstein was introduced to several filmmakers including Louis Delluc, Marcel L'Herbier, Germaine Dulac, and most importantly Abel Gance, who was recognized as the leader of what is now called the First French Film Avant-Garde or The French Narrative Avant-Garde to distinguish it from Dada and Surrealist filmmakers such as Man Ray and Luis Buñel. In 1923, because of his medical background, he was invited to shoot a documentary on Louis Pasteur, for the centenary of his birth, and his career as a filmmaker was launched. He made over twenty fiction films and an equal number of documentaries, many of which display remarkable technical innovations such as the photogenic close-up, quick or elliptical editing, slow and reverse motion, composite shots and sequences, sound manipulation, etc. Among his masterpieces are *A Faithful Heart* [*Coeur Fidèle*] (1923), *The Fall of the House of Usher* (1928), *Land's End* [*Finis Terrae*] (1930) and *The Storm-Tamer* [*Le Tempestaire*] (1947). These four films have only become available on tape or DVD over the last ten years, and the rest of his filmic *oeuvre* has yet to be re-released, most significant among these are his short poem-documentaries based on songs and the social documentaries he shot during the Front Populaire, the leftist government of France in the mid-1930s.

Although the main screening hall of the Cinémathèque Française bears his name (thanks to Marie Epstein who worked there until her death in 1994), for many years Epstein's filmic and theoretical work has suffered from acute critical neglect. Only one monograph on Epstein exists in French—it was written in 1964 by Pierre Leprohon—and besides a recent collection of essays that includes excerpts from his writings, no book concerning his films and theoretical writings has appeared in English, although a new monograph has since been published.[1] An extensive but incomplete edition of his theoretical works was published in 1974-75, and it profoundly influenced notable thinkers and theoreticians of cinema such as Gilles Deleuze and Jacques Rancière.[2] This translation of *L'intelligence d'une machine* is the first full-length book of Epstein's to appear in English.

L'intelligence d'une machine, published in 1946, was Epstein's tenth book, and his fourth dealing with cinema after *Bonjour cinéma* (1922), *Le Cinématographe vu de l'Etna* (1926), and *La Photogénie de l'impondérable* (1935). His first book, *La Poésie d'aujourd'hui, un nouvel état d'intelligence* (1921), dated from his years of writing poetry before his discovery of filmmaking, although in it he already argues that cinema had profoundly changed modernist literature. He also published *La Lyrosophie* (1922), an essay contrasting scientific and affective modes of knowing, two novels set in Brittany, *L'Or des mers* (1932), and *Les Recteurs et la sirène* (1934), and a treatise on homosexuality dating from the late 1930s, *Ganymède, essai sur l'éthique homosexuelle masculine*, which remains unpublished to this day.

The Intelligence of a Machine does not offer a theory of cinema, nor does it directly address the filmic concept with which Epstein's aesthetics have become quasi-synonymous: *photogénie*. As I explain elsewhere, *photogénie* denotes the sensations and emotions most characteristic of cinema as a medium for Epstein, that is, the ways in which the film-viewer experiences a particular shot or sequence all at once as a new face of reality, as material filmic images, and as affects evinced by both the medium and what it shows. *Photogénie* is thus a holistic experience of reality, mediation and the self all rolled into one.[3]

This holism is at the very heart of *The Intelligence of a Machine*, which may then be read as an expansion of *photogénie* toward philosophy. Yet it is not a book of philosophy in the traditional sense for several reasons. To begin with, the very attempt at basing a bona fide philosophical reflection on the cinema apparatus exceeds the genre, as it were, of established philosophical works ca. 1946. Indeed, only Deleuze seems to have understood what Epstein was up to in this book, which likely informed the inception of Deleuze's diptych on the philosophy of cinema in the 1980s. But also, while we are now used to the proliferation of monographs titled *The Philosophy of X,* where *X* is *The Matrix*, or *The Sopranos*, Epstein's book does the exact opposite. While such books illustrate established philosophical concepts using films as examples, *The Intelligence of a Machine* seeks to understand how cinema transforms our ways of thinking about ourselves, what we know, and the universe in a larger sense. In other words, it is truly a work on the philosophy *of* cinema in the nominative case, where cinema plays the part of the thinking agent. This explains why there is not a single movie referenced in the book. Finally, Epstein's philosophical culture and sources are disparate, yet *The Intelligence of a Machine* does not engage in any sustained way with philosophical scholarship. Although Epstein does mention Descartes, Leibniz, and Spinoza, he refers to them in the same way he does the Kabbalah and other hermetic writings. The one exception to this – though his name does not appear in the text – is Henri Bergson, who famously condemned the cinema on philosophical grounds, against whom Epstein argues insistently *in absentia* throughout the book. For Bergson, the essence of human life is duration, a qualitative experience of time that contrasts with the quantitative measure of time our watches give us. The cinema, Bergson asserts, by slicing duration into separate frames, re-quantifies time and thereby betrays human duration. Epstein radically disagrees with Bergson's analysis. One central argument of the book is that what the cinema in fact teaches us is that quantity is more fundamental than quality, or as he put it plainly in an unmistakable jab at Bergson in the title of chapter 8: "Quantity is the Mother of Quality."

The Intelligence of a Machine propounds positions that, as the reader will gauge, might appear rather extreme, such as the idea that filmic reverse motion shows that time's arrow itself is reversible, or that the only difference between organic life and inorganic stuff is the scale at, and movement through, which we observe them. There are different ways to deal with this difficulty. On the one hand, we might read the book not as a conventional philosophical treatise full of hyperbole, but as a kind of prolonged thought experiment about what happens to thought when we take cinema seriously: not as a mere tool of moving mimicry or a medium of expanded photographic representation, but as a source of absolutely new insights that challenge our epistemological presuppositions. A good deal of the lessons Epstein derives from cinema have to do with our social and cultural limitations, and as such, his challenge to the authority of scientific reason should be read as a pioneering attempt at cultural studies. Toward the end of the book, Epstein defines the notion of the apparatus (*le dispositif*) in ways that are strikingly prescient of Foucault's critique using the same term.

But we might also stay on scientific ground and follow Epstein's lead in connecting Einstein's theory of relativity and Heisenberg's uncertainty principle with cinema. Indeed, it would seem that the findings of more recent theoretical physics confirm many of Epstein's seemingly far-fetched intuitions. For example, the work of Nobel laureate physicist Kenneth Wilson focused on the crucial importance of scale in phase transitions of matter (between liquid and solid), and found a way to calculate the changing properties of physical laws at various scales of transition.[4] In *The Intelligence of a Machine* Epstein writes:

> In effect, space is flat or curved, matter is continuous or discontinuous, mechanics is determined or random, laws are causal or probabilistic, only in relation to the scale at which we study them: the average scale, or the infinitely small or big (73).

What seemed like a hyperbolic generalization of the whole universe in the way things in cinema appear to be different according to their difference of scale in film shots is in fact now confirmed by theoretical physics. Even time reversal, the central tenet of Epstein's philosophy of the cinema, has now been experimentally confirmed at the subatomic level by the BaBar experiments on meson decay at SLAC.[5] However, no knowledge of physics is needed to read *The Intelligence of a Machine*, but the reader would do well to keep in mind that while Epstein's meditations (on time, space, causality, scale, discontinuity, etc.) seem to defy common sense, they are far from non-scientific. Indeed, his book raises questions about time and space that are hotly debated in philosophy and science today.

The key philosophical lesson of this book is that if cinema's way of processing reality is taken seriously, it reveals that the universe is nothing like what we think it is. Cinema, as a philosophically pertinent experimental agent, casts radical doubt on human presuppositions about the major categories and concepts of time, space, being, substance, cause and effect, indeed it casts doubt upon the very notion of physical laws. Intriguingly then, Epstein comes very close to "speculative realism," a radical current in contemporary philosophy which argues—but from a purely logical perspective—a similar relativism regarding all human-centered physical laws.[6] However, a significant difference is that Epstein derives an abiding belief in interrelationism from cinema, that is, the idea that things such as space and time, which are apprehended as distinct by humans, are deeply connected by cinema as "thought," to the extent that the apparatus teaches us that everything is related. Thus Epstein does not at all share the premises held by speculative realists that relations—always understood as human-centered—conceal the meta-human singularity of objects. In fact, Epstein is a wonderful thinker and liberator of objects and body parts, which are not simply isolated in close-ups as part of a dramatic plot, but more importantly serve to disclose a new epistemology of affects crossing between human and non-human worlds. The more touching passages of the book have to do with the transitions cinema opens up between realms of being previously considered impervious to each other: humans, animals, plants, minerals and technologies. In the end Epstein is not a monadic thinker like Leibniz or Spinoza, nor a dualist like Descartes, nor a dialectical dualist like Hegel nor a holistic phenomenologist like Whitehead. He is a cine-existentialist, we might say, in that he wrote *The Intelligence of a Machine* at the apex of French existentialism, and instead of placing freedom and the absurd absence of a fixed reference system at the center of our life—as Sartre, Camus and Beckett did—he opted to recognize and trust the intelligence of a subaltern machine which had already wormed its way into the highest forms of thinking: cinema.[7]

While Abel Gance called Epstein "a young Spinoza," we might suggest a more Nietzschean subtitle for the book: *Intelligence of the Machine, or How to Philosophize with Cinema as a Fulcrum*. Epstein revered Nietzsche as a true freethinker, that is, a critic of accepted values and an iconoclast, and the two share an aphoristic, concise and trenchant style that spares no one—including themselves. *The Intelligence of a Machine* is mostly written in unadorned or direct French, though the original has a definite intensity, a rhythm of thought that informs some of its expressions and formulations with a kind of cadence, which at times can be difficult to translate. Epstein might appear to repeat himself at times: this is only a heuristic device to remind the reader of previous sections so they may follow the consequences he draws from them. Like Nietzsche, Epstein did not want to write philosophy in technical or ivory tower jargon, but in a language accessible to all who have a reasonable education and are interested in true thinking.

The film industry, by and large, see movies as commercial products and cinema as a powerful financial machine. Avant-garde filmmakers consider their movies to be art and cinema to be an important creative medium within human history. In this book, Epstein considers cinema to be a uniquely hybrid form of thinking whereby humans, for the first time, collaborate with the non-human to craft better presentations—not representations—of how the world and humans truly are. Although he often speaks of cinema's possibilities with a certain utopian reverence, Epstein is not a "believer" in cinema as a social or metaphysical solution. *The Intelligence of a Machine* propounds no creed other than a broad-minded lucidity toward what our world and our lives are actually made of when cinema thinks them with us.

Endnotes

1. Pierre Leprohon, *Jean Epstein* (Paris: Éditions Seghers, 1964); Christophe Wall-Romana, *Jean Epstein: Corporeal Cinema and Film Philosophy* (Manchester: Manchester UP, 2013); *The Cinema of Jean Epstein: Critical Essays and New Translations*, eds. Jason Paul and Sarah Keller (Amsterdam: University of Amsterdam Press, 2012).

2. Jean Epstein, *Écrits sur le cinema,* 2 vols. (Paris: Éditions Seghers, 1974, 1975).

3. Christophe Wall-Romana, *Jean Epstein: Corporeal Cinema and Film Philosophy* (Manchester: Manchester UP, 2013) 17-48.

4. "Kenneth Wilson, Nobel Physicist, Dies at 77," *The New York Times*, June 20, 2013.

5. "… at the particle level, time's arrow is not so easily defined. […] Thus the long wait for an unequivocal time-reversal violation in particle physics is finally over." Michael Zeller, "Viewpoint: Particle Decays Point to an Arrow of Time," *Physics* 5, 129 (2012). "For example, a particle traveling along some path with velocity to the left becomes a particle traveling along that path with velocity to the right, just like when we play a movie in reverse. Very simple." "How to Time-Reverse a Quantum System," Bryan W. Roberts, http://www.soulphysics.org/2009/11/how-to-time-reverse-quantum-system. Accessed on July 9, 2013.

6. See Translator's Endnote 11.

7. Jean-Paul Sartre, Albert Camus and Samuel Beckett were all three cinephiles who wrote film scenarios: Sartre even wrote a very Epsteinian short essay on cinema in his late teens. See my *Cinepoetry: Imaginary Cinemas in French Poetry*, 25-27.

Prefatory note:

Animated images bring out the components of a general representation of the universe, which tends to modify thought as a whole in various ways. Hence, very old, perennial problems—antagonisms between matter and mind, continuity and discontinuity, movement and stasis, or the nature of space and time, and the existence or inexistence of any reality—come into view under a brand new light.

A philosophy may then emerge from this play of light and shadow out of which, at first, spectators discern merely sentimental and comic plots.

The new images produced by astronomical instruments and microscopes have profoundly transformed and immensely stimulated all of human knowledge.

Will images created from this other optical system, this kind of robot-brain that is the cinematographic apparatus, have as great an influence upon the evolution of culture and civilization?

This question deserves to be asked.

The Intelligence of a Machine

Signs

Bewitched Wheels

A child sometimes notices, on screen, the images of a car driving at a constant speed, but whose wheels spin jerkily, now clockwise, now counterclockwise, even at times gliding without turning at all. Surprised, perhaps even worried by such a turmoil, the young observer might question an adult who, if he knows and cares, will account for this manifest contradiction, attempting to explain away this immoral instance of anarchy. More often, however, the questioner is content with an answer he doesn't really understand. Still, it might also come to pass that a twelve-year old philosopher from then on entertains a deep mistrust toward a spectacle displaying such a whimsical and perhaps fallacious picture of the world.

Uncanny Portraits

Disappointment, discouragement, these are the ordinary impressions of budding actresses, even the pretty and talented ones, when, for the first time, they behold and hear their own ghost at a screening. They find faults in their likeness they didn't think they had; they believe the lens and microphone have betrayed and robbed them; they neither recognize nor accept this or that feature of their face, this or that tone in their voice; before their doppelgangers, they each feel as if in the presence of a long lost sister, a stranger. The cinematograph lies, they say. Rarely does this lie appear to enhance or embellish.

Whether for good or not, in recording and reproducing a subject, the cinematograph always transforms it, recreates it as a second personality whose appearance might confound consciousness to the point of asking: who am I? Where is my true identity? And this represents a notable attenuation of the certainty that we exist, of our "I think therefore I am," to which we must add: "but I do not think myself the way I am."

The Personalism of Matter

The close-up further undermines the familiar order of appearances. The image of an eye, a hand, or a mouth filling up the entire screen—not only because it is magnified three hundred fold, but also because we see it severed from its organic community—acquires the autonomous character of an animal. Already, this eye, these fingers, these lips are beings, each possessing its own frontiers, its movement, its life, and its own ends. They exist unto themselves. It no longer seems to be a fable that there is a particular soul to the eye, the hand, or the tongue, as the vitalists[1] believed.

Inside the well of the eye's pupil, a spirit crafts its oracles. This immense gaze, one would like to touch it—if it weren't so laden with a possibly dangerous power. Nor does it appear to be a fable that light has a tangible mass. Within the egg of the eye's lens, a whole confused and contradictory world transpires, and in it we discern the universal monism of the Emerald Table again, the unification of what moves and is moved, the ubiquity of an unchanging life, the weights of thought and the spirituality of flesh.[2]

The Unity of Life

This upheaval in the hierarchy of things becomes more acute through the cinematographic reproduction of either accelerated or slowed down movements. Horses hover above an obstacle; plants gesticulate; crystals[3] couple, reproduce themselves and heal their wounds; lava slithers; water becomes oil, gum, pine pitch; man acquires the density of a cloud, the consistency of vapor; he has become a purely gaseous animal, with feline grace and ape-like dexterity. All the partitioned systems of nature are disarticulated. Only one realm remains: life.

In the case of gestures, even the most human ones, intelligence bows out to instinct which, alone, can direct the play of muscles, so subtle and nuanced, so blindingly true and happy. The whole universe becomes a giant beast whose stones, flowers, and birds are so many organs that cohere with precision in their participation as a single common soul. So many rigorous and superficial classifications presumed of nature are but artifices and illusions. Beneath this mirage, the multitude of forms [*le peuple des formes*] proves essentially homogeneous and strangely anarchic.

The Reversibility of the Universe

Innumerable experiences have paved the way for the dogma of life's irreversibility. Every evolution, in the atom or the galaxy, whether inorganic, animal or human, is sent on an irrevocable one-way trip by the dissipation of energy. The constant growth of entropy acts like a pawl preventing the cogs of the terrestrial and celestial machine from ever moving backwards. No time can return to its source; no effect can precede its cause. And a world that would aspire to free itself from this vectored order, or to modify it, would appear to be physically impossible and logically unimaginable.

Yet, it so happens that, in an old avant-garde film, in a burlesque comedy, we watch a scene that was registered backwards. And the cinematograph suddenly describes, with clear precision, a world that would go from its end to its beginning, an anti-universe that, previously, humanity could scarcely represent to itself. Dead leaves fly off the ground to perch themselves back onto tree branches; raindrops shoot up from the ground toward the clouds; a locomotive swallows its smoke and ashes, sucks in its vapor; a machine consumes the cold to provide energy and heat. A flower is born out of its decay and shrivels into a bud which retreats into the stem. In turn, the stem grows old and withdraws into the seed. Life emerges only through resurrection: it crosses and leaves behind the decrepitude of aging to reach the flowering of maturity; it devolves along its youth and childhood, only to dissolve into prenatal limbo. Here, universal repulsion, the degradation of entropy, and the constant growth of energy, represent truths that are inverse to Newton's law and the principles of Carnot and Clausius. The effect has become the cause; and the cause, the effect.

Could the structure of the universe be ambivalent? Could it allow both a forward and a backward movement? Could it admit a double logic, two determinisms, two opposite finalities?

The Cinema, an Instrument
Not Only for Art, but for Philosophy

Already for the last several centuries, microscopes and astronomical instruments have served to multiply the penetrating power of the primary sense of sight: the ensuing reflection upon these newly conquered aspects of the world prodigiously developed and transformed all the systems of philosophy and science. In all likelihood, the cinematograph, though it is only approximately fifty years old, is also starting to trigger important revelations, especially for the analysis of movement. Yet in the eyes of spectators the apparatus that begat the "seventh art" amounts to a machine renovating and vulgarizing theater, constructing a kind of spectacle accessible to the pocket books and minds of the largest international audience. This role, which is certainly beneficial and prestigious, nonetheless smothers, beneath the instrument's glory, other possibilities that end up escaping notice.

Hence, until now little attention has been devoted to the singularities that film representation can give of things: no one guessed that cinematographic images warn us of a monster, that they bear a subtle venom, capable of corrupting the whole reasonable order painstakingly imagined for the fate of the universe.

To discover always means to learn that objects are not what we thought they were: to know more requires, first of all, abandoning the most clear and certain part of established knowledge. It is not impossible—or unbelievable—that, as we watch moving images on a screen, what seems to us to be some kind of strange perversity, a surprising non-conformism, disobedience and error, might prove useful in order to proceed further into this "horrible underbelly things" which frightened even Pasteur's pragmatism.

The Interchangeability of Continuity and Discontinuity

A Kind of Miracle

As we know, a film comprises a large number of images juxtaposed on the filmstrip, and yet they are distinct and made somewhat dissimilar through the progressively modified position of the cinematographed subject. At a certain speed, the projection of this series of figures separated by short intervals of space and time produces the appearance of uninterrupted motion. Therefore the most striking wonder of the Lumière brothers' machine is precisely that it transforms a discontinuity into a continuity; that it allows for the synthesis of discontinuous and immobile elements into a mobile and continuous set; that it effects a transition between the two primordial aspects of nature which, ever since science and the metaphysics of science have existed, were strictly oppositional and mutually exclusive.

The First Semblance: Sensible Continuity

The scale at which our senses perceive the world, directly or indirectly, appears at first to be a rigorously coherent assemblage of material parts, in which the existence of an iota of nothingness, of any true discontinuity, seems so impossible that, in places where we do not know what there is, we have imagined a filler substance christened ether. Certainly, Pascal has demonstrated that the supposed horror of nature toward the void is a mirage, yet he did not dispel the horror that human intelligence feels toward the void, about which it can secure no sensorial experience.

Second Semblance:
Discontinuity in the Physical Sciences

Since Democritus, and against this primitive conception of universal continuity, the theory of atomism has victoriously developed itself through the presupposition that matter is constituted of indivisible corpuscles distant from one another. While the atom, in spite of its presumed indivisibility, had to be subdivided into several kinds of electrons, today we still generally accept the hypothesis of a discontinuous material structure with gaps, a gaseous structure one might say, both in the infinitely large and the infinitely small, in which the solid elements only occupy a very small volume compared to the immense vacuums through which they circulate. Hence a galaxy is compared to star vapor, in the same way that the atom recalls a miniature solar system.

Underneath the solid world that we know pragmatically hide surprises of a scattered reality in which the proportion of what is, in comparison to that which is not at all nameable, can be depicted by a fly aloft in a space of nearly one cubic mile.

Third Semblance: Mathematical Continuity

While material particles may be conceived of as distinct, they cannot be independently considered since they all exert reciprocal influences on each other that explain the behavior of every single one of them. The network of these innumerable interactions, or field of forces, represents an intangible weave that, for the proponents of Relativity, fills the entire space-time continuum. In this new four-dimensional continuity, energy, which is everywhere virtual, condenses itself here and there into granules possessing a mass: these are the elementary components of matter.

Underneath material discontinuity—whether molecular, atomic or subatomic—we must then imagine a continuity, deeper and still more hidden, that we might call pre-material since it prepares and directs the quanta and probabilistic locations of mass, light and electricity.

The Transmutation of Discontinuity into Continuity: Denied by Zeno, but Accomplished by the Cinematograph

The most obscure aspects of this poetry are to be found in the transitions and overlaps from superficial continuity to intermediate discontinuity, and thence to pre-material continuity whose existence remains strictly mathematical. That the same reality is able to cumulate continuity and discontinuity, that a series without rupture might be a sum of interruptions, that the addition of immobilities might produce movement, is what reason has puzzled over since the time of the Eleatics.

Yet, the cinematograph seems to be a mysterious mechanism devoted to assessing the false truth of Zeno's famous argument about the arrow, devoted to analyzing the subtle metamorphosis of stasis into mobility, of gaps into wholes, and of continuity into discontinuity, a transformation every bit as astounding as the generation of life out of inanimate matter.

Continuity, a Make-Believe Discontinuity

Is it the recording device or the projector that produces this marvel? In truth, all of the figures in each of the images of the film, successively projected on screen, remain as perfectly immobile and separate as they were when they emerged in the sensitive layer of the film. The animation and confluence of these forms does not take place on the filmstrip, or in the lens, but only within humans themselves. Discontinuity becomes continuity only once it has entered the movie-viewer. It is a purely interior phenomenon. Outside the viewing subject there is no movement, no flux, no life in the mosaics of light and shadow that the screen always displays as stills. But within ourselves, we get an impression that is, like all the other data of the senses, an interpretation of the object, that is to say, an illusion, a ghost.

Poor Sight Is the Source of the Metaphysics of Continuity

This phantom of a non-existing continuity, we know it is caused by a deficiency of our sight. The eye possesses a power of discrimination narrowly limited in space and time. A row of dots very close to one another is perceived as a line, evoking the ghost of spatial continuity. And a sufficiently quick succession of distinct but only slightly different images generates, because of the eye's lack of speed and retinal persistence, a new, more complex, and imaginary space-time continuity.

Every movie therefore gives us a clear instance of a mobile continuity that is only made, in its deeper reality, of immobile discontinuities. Zeno was thus right to argue that the analysis of movement provides a set of pauses: he was wrong only in denying the possibility of this absurd synthesis that actually recomposes movement by adding stoppages together, and which the cinematograph produces thanks to the weakness of our sight. "The absurd is not impossible," Faraday noted. The natural consequence of phenomena is not necessarily logical: we understand as much when, by adding light to light, we see darkness generated by interferences.

Is Discontinuity the Actuality of an Unreal Continuity?

Our continuous sensorium, whose daily experience assures us of the existence of everything around us, but whose actuality scientific research invalidates as a whole, ends up being a lie, born, like the fallacious continuity of a movie, of the insufficiency of the discriminating power not only of our sight, but of all our senses. Hence, the charm of music, a tightly linked flux of harmonies, which we enjoy when listening to a symphony, results from the inability of our hearing to distinctly locate each vibration of each set of sound waves in time and space. Hence, the relative coarseness of the multiple senses regrouped under the label of touch also allows us to know neither the minute divisions nor the formidable swarming of the most minuscule components in the objects we manipulate. It is out of the shortcomings of our perceptions that all the false notions of matter without gaps, of a compact world, or of a full universe are born.

At all levels, continuity, whether visible, touchable, audible, or breathable, is merely a first and very superficial appearance which likely has its use, that is, its practical truth, but which also masks a subjacent organization of a discontinuous nature whose discovery has proved remarkably useful, and whose degree of reality can, and consequently must, be held as deeper for the same reasons.

Discontinuity, a Make-Believe Continuity

Where does this discontinuity, deemed more real, come from? For instance, in the cinematographic apparatus, where and how are the discontinuous images the viewer uses to create the film's subjective continuity recorded? These images are taken from the perpetually moving spectacle of the world—a spectacle that is fragmented and quickly cut into slices by the shutter that unmasks the lens, at each rotation, for only a third or a quarter of the time that rotation takes. This fraction of time is so short that the resulting photographs are as sharp as snapshots of still subjects. The discontinuity and immobility of cinematographic frames, considered in themselves, are thus a creation of the camera apparatus, a very inexact interpretation of the continuous and mobile aspect of nature—an aspect standing for actual reality.

While Humans, Through Their Senses, Are Organized to Perceive Discontinuity as If It Were Continuity, the Apparatus, on the Contrary, "Imagines" Continuity More Easily as Discontinuity

In such an instance, a mechanism proves to be endowed with its own subjectivity, since it does represent things the way they are perceived by the human gaze, but only by the way it sees them, with its particular structure, which then constitutes a personality. And the discontinuity of still images (still at least during the time of projection, in the intervals between their abrupt substitution), a discontinuity acting as a real foundation to the imaginary human content of the projected film as a whole, ends up, in turn, being but a ghost, conceived and thought-out by an apparatus.

First, the cinematograph showed us, in continuity, a subjective transfiguration of a truer discontinuity; then, the same cinematograph shows us, in discontinuity, an arbitrary interpretation of a primordial continuity. We can presume, therefore, that neither cinematographic continuity nor discontinuity truly exist, or, conversely, that continuity and discontinuity alternatively act as object and concept, their reality being merely a function through which one can substitute for the other.

Continuity: Reality of an Artificial Discontinuity?

The entire discontinuity of the currently accepted scientific doctrine is no less artificial and deceitful than the discontinuity and immobility of cinematographic frames. Bernard Shaw refused to believe in either electrons or angels, since he had never seen either. If seeing was enough, the existence of electrons could not be doubted since, indeed, we can see them today, and count and measure them. However, it is far from certain that they exist in a natural state, in the course of the evolution of phenomena. All that can be posited is that they show up as results—monstrous ones perhaps—under certain experimental conditions that infringe upon and disfigure nature.

If we isolate one image of an actor's performance in a film recording, it might show the tensed-up face of the hero, his mouth twisted, one eye closed and the other upturned in a grotesque expression. Yet, during both the shooting and the projection, the scene appears well acted, moving, and without the slightest trace of comedy. But the camera apparatus, by fragmenting the continuity of the gestures of a protagonist, cuts out a discontinuous image of the scene, which because of its very discontinuity, is false, and will regain its truth only when it reenters its original continuity during the projection.

In the same way, the powerful instruments used by physicists intrude within material, apparent or deep continuity, in order to cut it up into billions of pieces, and the result of this brutal surgery, of these firings and dismemberments, transmutations and explosions, are discontinuous aspects: atoms, protons, electrons, neutrons, photons, quanta of energy, etc., which perhaps, more than likely, did not exist before the destructive experiments on continuity. A spinthariscope, a cyclotron, or an electronic microscope extracts a few snapshots from out of the texture of the universe, transplanting them into space, fixing them in time—yet these winces of tortured nature have no more real signification than the happenstance of a comical expression attributed to the mask of a tragic actor.

We break a pane of glass, count its pieces, and proclaim: this pane of glass was composed of four triangular pieces, two rectangular ones and six pentagons, etc. This is the model of reasoning of all atomistics, indeed similar to that of Zeno. Nonetheless, it is clear that the pane of glass, before it splintered into pieces, was composed of no triangles, rectangles or pentagons, nor any other pieces, but was only the unity it constituted.

Reality: A Sum of Unrealities

Some analyses of light show it to have a granular, discontinuous structure. But it is impossible to demonstrate that this discontinuity existed prior to the investigative experiments that generated it, in the same manner that the camera apparatus invented a succession of pauses within the continuity of a movement. Other phenomena concerning light may be explained only if light is considered as an uninterrupted flux of waves, rather than a continuity of projectiles. Wave mechanics has not entirely succeeded in erasing this incomprehensible contradiction, by assuming that light rays have a double nature, immaterially continuous and materially discontinuous, formed of a corpuscle and a pilot wave, about which, all we can know is its mathematical formula, which determines the probabilities according to which the grain of light materializes here rather than there.

Confronted with an insoluble problem, an irreconcilable contradiction, we might do well to suspect that in fact, there is neither problem nor contradiction. The cinematograph instructs us that continuity and discontinuity, rest and movement, far from being two incompatible modes of reality, are two interchangeable modes of unreality, twin "ghosts of the mind" as Francis Bacon called them, seeking to purge knowledge at the cost of leaving nothing in it. Everywhere, sensible continuity and mathematical continuity, these ghosts of human intelligence, may substitute or be substituted for the discontinuity intercepted by machines—the ghost of mechanical intelligence. They are no more mutually exclusive than the colors of a disk and the whiteness that results when it spins. Continuity and discontinuity, rest and movement, color and whiteness, alternatively play the role of reality, which is here as elsewhere, never, nowhere, merely a function, as we will make clear later on.

Non-Temporal Time

Learning Perspective

Any spectacle that imitates a series of events, by the sheer fact of the successiveness it contains, creates its own time as a deformation of historical time. In primitive theatrical performances this false time strayed as little as possible from the actual span of time it took for the described action. Similarly, early draftsmen and painters ventured only with diffidence into false relief, not knowing how to counterfeit spatial depth very well as they were still beholden to the reality of the flat surface on which they worked. It was only progressively that humans, developing their genius at being the imitative animal par excellence, going from imitations of nature to secondary and tertiary imitations of these first tries, became used to fictive time and space, straying ever further from their original models.

Hence the length of mystery plays in the Middle Ages translates the unease that people still felt about altering temporal perspective in this period. In such an era, a drama that did not last as long on stage as the unfolding of real facts would have neither been believed nor have any power of illusion. The rule of the three units that allowed for twenty-four solar hours to be compressed into a performance that lasts three or four hours marks a new stage of achievement toward understanding chronological shortcuts, that is, temporal relativity. Today, this one-eighth reduction of duration, the maximum permitted by classical tragedy, seems like a minimal effort compared to the compressions at the $1/50,000^{th}$ obtained by the cinematograph, even though these make us somewhat dizzy.

The Time-Thinking Machine

Another astounding merit of the cinematograph is that it multiplies and immensely softens the play of temporal perspective, training the mind for a gymnastics that isn't always easy: switching from an inveterate absolute to unstable conditionals. Here too, this machine that stretches or condenses duration, demonstrating the variable nature of time, preaching the relativity of all measures, appears to be endowed with a psyche. Without it, we would see nothing of what time might feel like materially when it is fifty thousand times faster or four times slower than that in which we live. Certainly, the machine is a concrete tool but its workings provide such a sophisticated semblance to the human mind, and conform to the mind's own uses so well, that we must consider it a half-thinking: a form of thinking by the rules of analysis and synthesis that, without the cinematographic apparatus, humans would have been incapable of implementing.

Dimensions of Space

Although the respect that we take in preserving irradiated platinum in tabernacles at a controlled temperature, reinforced and locked, recalls the cults of old that formed around miraculous items considered as materializations of revealed certainty fallen from the celestial absolute into our world of errors, no one considers the meter—the ten millionth part of a quarter of the terrestrial meridian—to be an intangible and essential truth. Many countries still use other units of measure. Everyone has long since witnessed four millimeters becoming three and half centimeters under a magnifying glass. Travelers know that a kilometer always presents different values, depending on whether travel is by foot, on horseback, on a bicycle, in a car, a train, or a plane, and according to the terrain, the climate and the season. Like the meters of the moon, Mars, or Venus—the ten millionth part of a quarter of the meridian of our satellite or these planets—the terrestrial meter has only a relative signification. And if these celestial bodies, as we believe, contract themselves, we have to wonder where our true meter may be: in the less variable standards of the Bureau des Longitudes or in the subdivision of a perpetually shrinking meridian?

Dimensions of Time

The truth-value of an hour, though more mysterious, would seem less subject to suspicion. The hour is not merely the product of secret standard clocks, buried and religiously venerated in deep vaults; nor is it the simple result of some measure of the globe's surface: it was born on solar dials from the trace inscribed by the incomprehensible and divine movement animating the whole celestial machine. While the meridian lends itself, haphazardly, to a decimal division, the ellipse of the orbit refuses to submit itself to the arbitrariness of this human contrivance. It imposes its own number of days and nights so tyrannically that, although this counting is wobbly and we haven't succeeded in fixing it, calendars must constantly adjust to it. At times, certainly, an hour of boredom appears to flow more slowly than an enjoyable hour, but these impressions, always confused and contradictory, are not enough to shake our faith in the inexorable fixity of the universal rhythm. This belief is confirmed yet again by the invariably positive irreversibility of duration, an image of the irreversible constancy of astronomical movements, whereas space, in its length, width and depth, may be measured any which way. Hence, until the cinematograph's invention of accelerated motion and slow motion, no one had even thought about the possibility of seeing one year in the life of a plant condensed into ten minutes, or thirty seconds of close-up activity of an athlete spread over two minutes.

Time Is a Spatial Relation

Hence the hour together with the time it defines, born and regulated by cosmic dynamics, appeared to have quite a different reality than that of the meter and space: at once more obscure, more elevated, intangible and immutable. Yet the cinematograph, by laminating time and showing its extreme malleability, took it down from these heights and reduced it to a dimension analogous to that of space.

The fourth dimension has been talked about for a long time, though it was difficult to imagine what it could be, and easy to doubt it existed at all. For some mathematicians it essentially amounted to a geometric dimension like the other three—as a fiction or a reality of calculus—but in practice it is ungraspable since our senses provide no data about it. For many scientists and novelists, philosophers and poets, it was the ether, or a means to reach the stars, the dwelling of pure spirits or the means to resolve the squaring of the circle…. However, because many things humans often think about end up becoming real, the fourth dimension—like this unicorn finally captured in Nepal—ultimately showed up, with the gift of verisimilitude, in the space-time continuum of the proponents of relativity.

Time, understood as a scale of variables, as the fourth in the system of coordinates inscribed within our representation of the universe, would still have remained a figment of the mind, satisfying only a narrow circle of scientists, if the cinematograph had not visualized this conception and reinforced it by experimentally producing wide variations until then unknown from a temporal perspective. That our time is the framework of a variable dimension, in the same way as our space is the place for three kinds of relative dimensions, can now be understood by everyone because we can now see the lengthening or shortening of time on screen, in the same way as we see the lengthening or shortening of a distance at either end of a pair of binoculars. If, today, the least cultivated person may represent for himself the universe as a four-dimensional continuum in which all material accidents may be located using four space-time variables; if this finer, more mobile and truer figure progressively supplants the three-dimensional image of the world, in the same manner that the latter was substituted for flat primitive schematizations of earth and sky; if the indivisible unity of the four factors of space-time is slowly acquiring the evident nature attributed to the inseparability of the three dimensions of pure space—then all this is due to the cinematograph, this penetrating vulgarization machine. And all the profits go to the theory to which the names of Einstein and Minkowski have principally been linked.

Fourth or First Dimension?

Nevertheless, the three dimensions of space, between themselves, only present differences of position that are in no way essential, the temporal dimension retains its own character, which at first is attributed to the irreversible march of time, on the other hand, movements along the three other dimensions are considered reversible. Yet since the four dimensions constitute inseparable co-variants of each other, it would seem strange that one could be irreversible without forcing the other three to be so as well. In truth, no body in motion, living or inanimate, can ever undo the way it has traveled. The return kilometer does not annul the first kilometer traveled, but adds to it, as a new kilometer, different from the first. The night route, even if it does not vary an inch from the morning route, is always another route, with another light, in another air, with another heart and other thoughts. The irrevocable march of time impresses a one-way direction to all of the universe's movements, an irrecoverable and indestructible value, perpetually positive. The *sui generis* quality of the temporal dimension is its power to orient geometric space in such a way that successions can only take place according to the direction of this polarity. Similarly, it is from the polarized movement it brings to images that the cinematograph—once it is stereoscopic—gives us a perfect illusion of the four-dimensional continuum as if it were a new reality.

Instead of sticking to a chronological order, in which humans became familiar with the measures of length, surface, volume and duration, should we not call the time value the first dimension instead—not the fourth—to acknowledge the general directional role it exerts on space?

Local and Incommensurable Times

The cinematograph not only explains that time is a directed dimension, correlative to those of space, but also that every estimate of this dimension only has a particular value. We recognize that astronomical givens, those of the Earth, impose an aspect and a division of time quite different from what they must be in the Andromeda galaxy, whose sky and movement are not the same; seen from the outside, it is difficult for those who have never seen the accelerated motion or slow motion of the cinematograph to imagine the appearance of a time other than our own. A short documentary describing, in a few minutes, twelve months of the life of a plant, from its germination to its maturity and its withering, up to the forming of the seeds of the new generation, is enough to make us accomplish the most fantastic voyage, the most difficult escape, that humans have ever attempted.

Such a film seems to free us from terrestrial time, that is, solar time, a time that we felt nothing would ever liberate us from. We feel we are presented with a new universe, a new continuum, whose movement through time is fifty thousand times faster. There, in this tiny realm, reigns a particular time, a local time, representing a small enclave within terrestrial time—though it too, spread over a large area, is merely a local time, in turn inserted within other times, or else juxtaposed, or mixed, with them.

The time of the whole universe itself is merely a particular time, valid for this whole but not beyond it, or any of its inner provinces.

Only by analogy can we get an inkling of these innumerable ultra-particular times that give shape to these atomic ultramicrocosms which wave or quantum mechanics assume to be incommensurable to each other, in the same way that they have no common measure with solar time.

Time Is Not Made of Time

Fed by the senses, it is only with difficulty that our intelligence weans itself from its primitive conception of a sensible continuum. In the same way it filled up space with ether, it endowed time with some manner of consistency, however slight, corresponding to the vague fluidity of ordinary perceptions of duration bestowed by coenesthesis.[4] This exquisite fabric, this tenuous thread of the Fates, this dwindling film [*pellicule de chagrin*],[5] this unsettled substance, more subtle than ether and refusing to even bear a proper name, remained nonetheless a material reality.

The cinematograph has destroyed this illusion: it shows time to be merely a perspective resulting from the succession of phenomena, the way space is merely a perspective of the coexistence of things. Time contains nothing we might call time-in-itself, no more so than space comprises space-in-itself. They are made, one and the other, of essentially variable relationships among appearances that occur in succession or in simultaneity. This is why there can be thirty-six different times and twenty kinds of space, in the same way there can be innumerable particular perspectives according to the infinitely diverse positions of objects and observer.

Thus, after having taught us about the unreality of both continuity and discontinuity, the cinematograph rather abruptly ushers us into the unreality of space-time.

Neither Spirit Nor Matter

The Measure of God?

In the Trismegistus[6] we read that priests of ancient Egypt spent their nights piously measuring, against the vault of the heavens, the variations of divine majesty that they calculated in units of *atrui*. It would appear to be an absurd irreverence—if there is a God—that the infinite ubiquity and perfect spirituality of the universal principle should have been held as measurable and variable. However, the cinematograph, showing us the functional relativity and the deep community of continuity and discontinuity, may also lead us to surmise the relativity and unity of another couple ordinarily thought to be split across an essential antagonism: matter and spirit.

Time Acceleration Increases Life and Spirit

The sheer gamut of the plays of space-time perspective achieved by accelerated motion and slow motion, as well as close-ups, trigger the discovery of movement and life in what was held to be immutable and inert. In an accelerated projection, the scale of the realms of being shifts—to some degree, according to acceleration—in the direction of a more qualified existence. Hence, crystals start

27

vegetating like live cells; plants become animal, choosing their lighting and support and expressing their vitality through gesticulations.

It is less surprising to us if we recall certain experimental results obtained by patient researchers. For instance, the mimosa has been trained against its habit to spread its leaves at night and curl them during the day. Vegetal movements that our gaze hardly discerns in human time are hence revealed by the gaze of the lens thanks to the cinematographic contractions of time which allow us to observe within plants the cooperation of two faculties generally considered to be characteristic of animals: sensibility and memory, through which a judgment of purposefulness or harmfulness is exercised. We might then keep from smiling at the botanist studying the psychology of orchids, since a substance displaying memory of its own malleability is certainly on the way toward possessing something akin to spirit. Similarly, certain kinds of paramecia trained to twirl counter to their natural movement, and to eat or fast according to the color of light they're exposed to, testify to the fact that they benefit from learned experience, that is to say, they can govern themselves intelligently. It is in the exercise of such intelligence that "the seed, by developing into a plant, pronounces its judgment," as Hegel writes, and that "the egg (in developing into a mature form) obeys its memory," or its logic and duty, as Claude Bernard professed—a vitalist and Hegelian in his own fashion.

The Slowing Down of Time
Increases Death and Matter

Conversely, during a slow motion projection we observe a degradation of forms as they undergo a diminution of their mobility and thus lose their vital quality. Human semblance, for instance, is deprived in large part of its spirituality. Thought vanishes in the human gaze and becomes numb and illegible upon the face. In gestures, awkwardness—a sign of will and the ransom of freedom—disappears, absorbed by the infallible grace of animal instinct. The whole human body is but a being of smooth muscle swimming in a dense medium, in which thick currents always carry and shape this clear descendant of old marine fauna and maternal waters [*eaux-mères*].[7] Regression reaches even further, beyond the animal stage. It rediscovers, in the movements of the torso or the neck, the active elasticity of the stem; in the undulating of hair or a horse mane, the swaying of a forest; in the beating of fins and wings, the palpitating of leaves; in the coiling and uncoiling of reptiles, the spiral sense of all vegetal growth. Slowed down even more, any living substance goes back to its fundamental viscosity and lets its deep colloidal nature rise to the surface. Finally, when there is no longer any visible movement in a sufficiently stretched time, humans become statues, the living merges with the inert, the universe devolves into a desert of pure matter without any trace of spirit.

Life is a *Trompe-l'œil* of Time

Thus, if we accelerate the rhythm of time, increasing the world's mobility, we let more life transpire or we create more of it; and if, conversely, we slow down the course of time, curbing the movement of beings, we cause the disappearance or destruction of their vital quality.

For vitalists who located life pretty much everywhere but found it nowhere, it was a quasi-divine principle, the essence of essences. For biochemists, it is the exquisite result of highly complex molecular reactions. Analyzed by the cinematograph, life presents itself foremost as a function of temporal rhythm: it is the correlative of a certain minimal speed of movements, below which nothing living can transpire.

However, apart from the rhythm of succession, nothing has changed in the nature of a crystal promoted to the living by accelerated motion, in the same way that nothing would have changed if the local time of the screen had replaced normal terrestrial time with a more widespread temporal zone. Inert, then alive, alive and dead, the crystal remains precisely the unknown thing that it was. It receives and loses life, without modifications to its mysterious reality. Life is a spectrum whose first characteristic is mathematical, since it results from numerically determined proportions between the intervals of a series of events. When certain cadences are or become perceptible to the senses, we feel them and judge them to be alive, similar to the way we see a limited spectrum as luminous in the whole series of electro-magnetic vibrations. The accelerated motion of the cinematograph discloses the fact that, within the immensity of non-life, there is still and always will be life—ordinarily imperceptible life—in the same way that the photo-cell discloses that there is still light in infrared wavelengths: black light.

"Spontaneous Generation" Through Mutation of Time

Here we can see the problem of "spontaneous generation" in a brand new light. Pasteur's negative demonstration, at once too materialistic and too scholastic, as has often been said, proves almost nothing on one side or the other. Perhaps it is because there was nothing to prove in this realm of thought. Cinematographic acceleration can fabricate life with minerals, miles of footage. It is merely a semblance, one will object. Yet what is not merely a semblance?

Were we located and organized so as to perceive a faster time—such as we occasionally envision in dreams—hundreds of crystal species would no doubt appear to be just as alive as bacteria or protozoa. If in the movements of the universe, or one of its provinces, a change in rhythm occurred, a modification of local times, the whole Earth would seem to us covered with billions of new lives, "spontaneously generated." In a world where everything ultimately proves to be relative and variable, it would be surprising to find that time ratios are perennial constants. Time has evolved too, evolves and probably will keep on evolving, but so slowly in comparison to our own duration that this variation remains ungraspable to us. Hence today humans believe that they have discovered viruses through their own means of investigation—these relatively huge molecules that seem to be hybrid forms to us, unstable and hesitant, on the threshold of inorganic and organic being, of life and the inanimate. But is this discovery not instead the work of the slow evolution of time that accelerates, which is to say, animates matter, producing "spontaneous generation" under the microscope of scientists? An observer who would have lived through all the centuries since the formation of our planet, as if they were minutes, might have recorded innumerable advents of life caused only by the accelerated action of the progressive change of time upon a material that is in itself unchanged.

We have admitted for a long time now—even if we prefer to deny it—that "spontaneous generation" or rather the continuity of all forms of nature, is inscribed in the human logic of things as necessarily as the existence of an invisible planet was embedded in the calculations of Leverrier.[8] The realm of thought calls for facts more than it stems from them. Neptune could not not be, by the same token that "spontaneous generation" had to be or must have been. What is surprising is to encounter it, not under the form of a biochemical novelty, but as a mutation of temporal perspectives.

The Soul, the Mind, and Instinct: Functions and Fictions of the Time Variable

Although everyone has their own particular understanding or misunderstanding of what could or could not be the living and the inanimate, matter and spirit, body and soul, almost all concur that the inert is thought to be only material, while beings sufficiently endowed with a vital quality are bestowed the privilege of also developing a spiritual quality, which reveals itself all the more clearly as forms become more complex, from animals to humans. Spirit is thus an aristocratic corollary of matter.

While psychic functions do not project on screen with as much clarity as vital functions, we nonetheless have seen that the acceleration and slowing down of time acts on both, as we logically surmise, in an analogous way: accelerated motion, at the same time that it intensifies life, uncovers a quasi vegetal soul among minerals, a quasi animal soul among plants, while slow motion, which disanimates and devitalizes beings, erases the most human expression in people, fostering in them the return and domination of the tried and true harmony of instinctual gestures.

Therefore, to go from more or less matter to more or less spirit, to traverse all the degrees that separate the blind will of the stone, named gravity, to the tendencies [*tendances*] of an undecipherable complexity called states of mind, all that is needed is to move along the scale of time. All that is needed is to artificially create a time in which each minute is worth two hundred of our seconds for intelligence to seem occulted, regressing toward instinct; or a time in which each second comprises ten of our hours in order for crystals to reveal their instincts, and plants their dialectics. There is no more of an essential difference or insurmountable barrier between matter and spirit than there is between the living and the non-living. The same profoundly unknown truth manifests itself as alive or inanimate, endowed or devoid of soul, according to the duration through which it is considered. As with lives, there can also be "spontaneous generations" of spirit, produced by the mere variation of temporal dimensions.

Dimensional Limits of Evident Truths

Depending on the dimensions of a series of events in time, life or soul reveals itself or does not, exists or does not. What figures as indisputably alive and highly spiritual within our centimeter-gram-second system of reference, would no doubt figure as inert and exclusively material in another system of reference, in which the value of the time unit would markedly differ. In fact, the most evident of our principles, the most certain of our realities only possess evidence and certainty relative to the dimensions of the system within, for, and through which they were conceived.

Everyone knows today that Euclid's postulates, which our reason hardly succeeds in putting into doubt, are nonetheless true only at the very limited scale of human architecture. These are truths of civil engineers. Merely transposed to the scale of the whole globe, calculated with tens of thousands of kilometers rather than meters, reduced to the ten-millionth in the visual field these clear and distinct evidences are proven false. We then notice that parallel lines necessarily meet, whereas according to Euclid they cannot. The same straight lines which are parallel in an order of magnitude from one to a hundred thousand meters are also converging and curving lines within a representation in which each centimeter figures ten thousand terrestrial kilometers, as we can witness in any atlas. Other perspectives, contractions or extensions of space, could make us surmise, still within those lines, spirals or cycloids enmeshed in an indescribable and unimaginable way.

It is useless, however, to wonder what these "mix-lines," in Montesquieu's expression, whether straight or curved, parallel or intersecting, might really be. There exist as many apparent, dissimilar and often contradictory realizations of those lines as there are different more or less extended spaces we can conceive of. That is to say that there are no figures that can be absolutely, in themselves, flat or curved, tangent or perpendicular, oblique or vertical.

Similarly, nothing exists, according to its own intrinsic virtue, as living or inert, spirit or matter. Something whose essence remains completely inaccessible to us is in turn angel and beast, plant and mineral, depending on the conditions of space and time in which they occur. Life and death, body and soul, these are merely labels of the inter-convertible perspectives serving as guises to the same unnamable and unthinkable thing that is perhaps merely a function or a conjecture as well.

But Flesh Also Becomes Verb

When what it is, has not yet condensed into granules of matter, it exists in a pre-material phase we presume to be pure energy. So long as it remains immaterial, the only other way it can be conceived of is as a kind of spiritual state. Hence, in the most intimate depth of things in which thought may descend, we discover that spirit forms the essential constituent of matter.

At the other end of the imaginable, at the summit of the most complex and heaviest molecular organizations, appears the psyche, the soul, that is to say, again, spirit.

Issued from spirit, matter returns to it, in the course of a cycle whose two transmutations are the two great, the two absurd mysteries of scientific faith. To eschew the embarrassment of such enigmas, some believe only in the reality of matter, others in that of spirit. Yet the cinematograph lets us surmise that there is no more reality in material aspects than in spiritual appearances; that we can mechanically cross over from the former to the latter, or vice versa, through simple time contractions or extensions. Probably, since these two kinds of forms can also coexist within the same local time, they must each correspond, to some particular modality of the X that is their common source, though these differences cannot be essential. Through the prism of time, the X produces a threefold spectrum: pre-material spirit, matter, and post-material spirit, all of which are merely the same X, just like sunlight forms the eighty or so hues of the rainbow that are nothing but light. By developing this analogy, we can also notice that the displacement of bodies in the space-time continuum shifts their light spectrum proportionally to their speed, either toward the red or the violet, in the same way as it shifts their substantial spectrum toward either material or spiritual values.[9]

The Randomness of Determinism
and the Determinism of Randomness

The Anarchy of Spirit
and the Servitude of Matter

The highest form of spirit, the soul, attributed to the highest manifestations of life, was for a long time, and unanimously, considered to be endowed with a marvelous privilege: the power to freely exercise its will, that is to say, to exercise it in a completely anarchic way. While recent psychology has succeeded in raising scientific doubt over the supposed independence of the human person, moral liberty not only remains the dogma theoretically professed by the great religions (in spite of their counter-dogmas on grace and predestination), but it is practically used by all social systems forced to affirm the responsibility of the individual.[10]

Conversely, even the most inveterate spiritualists recognize—at times to such a degree that they prove quite libertarian concerning people—that the domain of the inert, as that of the simplest forms of life, is exclusively ruled by the rigorous determinism which so many sciences have happily benefitted from for their development.

Nevertheless, as materialistic or deterministic as these scientists may be, in their investigations of the deepest level of pure matter they have surprisingly discovered that the chain of cause and effect, seen

37

everywhere as precise and complete, has recently suffered some strange lapses in those realms. Inside the atom, as established in Heisenberg's famous equations, determinism crumbles: the object ceases to be precisely identified and located, the phenomenon refuses to let itself be entirely predicted in space and in time at once. Within the pre-matter there is a sort of spirit that appears as a kind of freedom and disorder: chance.

The universe—made of a discontinuity located between two continuities, a material realm bordered by two immaterial realms, a zone of determinism lodged between two zones of indetermination—presents itself, thrice, as a tripartite construction in which the similitude of extreme parts—alchemy taught us "that which is above is like that which is below; that which is below is like that which is above"—might evoke the image of cycles. Within such cycles the cinematograph lets us surmise the fundamental unity of forms reputed to be irreconcilable but which, through this apparatus, may be automatically converted, one into another. Because matter thereby becomes spirit, and continuity discontinuity, and vice versa, we must also expect that chance, determinism and freedom might uncover, beneath their superficial contradictions, a deep equivalence corresponding to the essential homogeneity of the material and spiritual aspects of things and beings.

Chance Results Not from an Absence of Determination but an Excess of Determination

The word chance is nonsensical in the generally accepted sense of the term, the freedom with which events occur unconditionally as if of their own accord: no occurrence of chance understood as such has ever presented itself to everyday experience. Our understanding is indeed constituted so that it cannot conceive of a phenomenon without a cause. Even a miracle or a wonder requires determination, from God or the Devil. As soon as our intelligence analyzes them, any event or act appears to us as inevitably preceded and followed by certain other conditions or conjunctures. In the same way that through a red-tinted glass we see red everywhere, through our reason we see reasons for everything everywhere.

And often, we see too many reasons. When these are so numerous and entangled that it becomes difficult to master their interactions and calculate their exact consequences, we call their effects random. Randomness is not characterized by essential gratuity and spontaneity, which we still cannot grasp: it results only from our practical powerlessness at predicting an event whose nature is nonetheless as perfectly determined as that of all the others. The world at the human scale is full of unpredictability but comprises nothing inherently unpredictable. Hence, by a minute analysis of the mass, movement and friction of the initial position of the balls of a lottery, one or several generations of scientists should inevitably succeed in establishing, through mechanical laws, the winning numbers of the lottery in a given drawing. Only the cost and length of such a project render it unrealizable, so that the formation of wealth-giving numerical combinations—though anyone can see it is merely the solution of a pure problem of physics—continues to be attributed to the whimsy of a chimera: chance.

Far from introducing arbitrariness, in which our organic nature has a hard time believing, chance itself is introduced, that is to say, determined by an excessive causality obscuring itself through its own superabundance.

Chance is but the illusion of overly complex determinations.

Heisenberg's Equations:
a Prelude to True Chance?

Nevertheless, at the scale of the constituents of the atom, in the infinitely small, chance presents itself with a particular character. It is no longer a matter, as with human dimensions, of phenomena whose determinants which, though they cannot be practically calculated, are of such a nature that they could eventually become entirely and simultaneously known. In subatomic mechanics we are dealing with semblances whose determinants essentially cannot, even purely theoretically, be recorded at the same moment. The more we know the position of a photon in space, the less it is possible to measure its quantity of movement, and vice versa. Two groups of data, conjointly required to fully determine a corpuscle, undergo, in our mind, a strange law of oscillation that only allows them to reach their full precision through alternation. This mysterious rhythm seems to dissociate and oppose space and time, which here tend to only become knowable when they are separated from each other. There is an incorrigible limp within mathematical formulas themselves: either they provide the movement of a projectile they cannot exactly locate, or they define its placement, leaving its energy of movement unknown. Such uncertainties might give us an inkling of true chance—in fact the only known example of it. True chance, no longer as an unpredictability of fact but of principle; incalculability no longer by virtue of excess but by sheer absence of determinants.

Subatomic Chance:
the Deception of Another Determinism

Yet, experience shows us that this authentic arbitrariness we think we detect in the ultra-microcosm obeys certain laws: the law of probability, a law that also governs the deceptive randomness of the world is actually determined at the human scale. In fact, the existence of any one of these laws—that of Bernouilli, for instance—is enough to logically establish that the fundamental postulate of "the independence of probabilities" is a myth, since it is clear that if any law may be applied to a series of events, it then registers the functioning of a relation among them, which necessarily excludes any so-called independence.

Independence, just like the trivial randomness of life, is merely a semblance and a practical truth. For a player, each result of flipping a coin—heads or tails—may appear independent of preceding results, because considered in itself or in very small series, it is materially unpredictable. But if this discontinuity was absolutely true, ten consecutive tosses resulting in heads would be just as probable as any other streak of heads within ten coin tosses, whether five or four or six. But everyone knows this isn't the case, as the law of intervals dictates. It is only the coin toss that is about to occur whose result is indeed unpredictable in ordinary conditions of play that interests and occupies the gambler's mind so imperiously that it dominates and erases the more abstract notion of an order, predictable and predicted, linking all the results in a series. The tyranny of the present, forcing us to judge all things according to their most direct utility or uselessness, creates the false evidence of the independence of probabilities, the twin of the false evidence of the parallelism of vertical lines. In logic, if there are laws, there cannot be independence of facts, and without independence, it becomes impossible to argue for true chance.

Within the atom as well as outside it, the freedom of facts is nothing more than a myth that seems to cloak either normal but superabundant determinations at the human scale, or a still-mysterious form of determinism at the subatomic scale. Its analysis might require a multiplication and dissociation of space-time coordinates. We would discover minute and formidable monsters there: crowding the voids of matter, universes of a trillion trillionth of a cubic millimeter, highly multidimensional, each determined from within by several directions of time and even more so of space.

Determinism:
an Aberrant Consequence of Chance

Suppose we conceive of our universe as being determined as little as possible and therefore almost abandoned to true chance. The molecules of a fluid would freely circulate in it and, since they are infinitely numerous, since they have no reason for going in one direction rather than another, since they hit each other more often where they are the least scattered, they end up populating the entirety of space. Moreover—and this is a simple fact all pool players know from experience without needing to seek out another cause—during their disorderly contacts, these particles automatically exchange and level their kinetic energy which, originally, could be arbitrarily dissimilar. We therefore understand that in merging two receptacles containing fluids at different pressure and temperature, by the mere anarchic and spontaneous mixing of molecules, both receptacles will inevitably strike a balance of mean pressure and temperature. From an absence of law was born a law, not the least of them, defining the behavior of certain states of matter. It is a false law or, as we put it, a statistical law—a law of pure chance. It merely indicates that it is infinitely probable that things will behave in this manner, because there is not one chance in a billion they will behave otherwise. But it isn't absolutely impossible that one of the very rare contrary eventualities will occur, so that, for instance, all the particles more full of energy will assemble themselves in one of the two receptacles, combining their temperature and pressure.

When we examine them closely, all the laws we know and trust to be causal are in fact, directly or indirectly, only probable laws. Some of these probabilities are so strong that in thousands and thousands of millennia, no discrepancy would occur. From such a long atavistic experience, we draw our quasi-certainties, our faith in determinism. The latter is but the vulgar, superficial, and utilitarian aspect of the supposed organization of the universe that might as well be the work of chance and continue to exist, as it will disintegrate, by chance alone.[11]

Psychic Chance or Freedom,
the Other End of Classic Determinism

As in the case of material and spiritual semblances, the deterministic perspective depends upon the dimension of phenomena. It becomes murky at the infinitesimal scale of the components of the atom, in the mechanics of Planck, de Broglie and Bohr; it also gets muddled, at the other end of the chain of observable forms, at the level of the more complex and heaviest of molecular structures that generate life and thought beholden to physiology and psychology; it only governs an intermediate zone, above all the domain of classical physics and chemistry that corresponds to relatively simple atomic assemblages of average mass and size.

The psychic eclipse of determinism—which under the name of freedom usually passes for the noblest privilege of the soul—nonetheless occurs under the same conditions as those resulting from the most common chance: a large number of entangled and subtle causes. Because, in the majority of cases, it is impossible to analyze, whether subjectively or objectively, the whole network of motives, the whole field of forces, from which the least of our acts results, this act appears as though governed by a will beyond the law, sovereign, god-given, and unchecked. Naive considerations of self-respect and the necessities of social organization confirm this faith in the myth of moral autonomy and personal responsibility, linked to the biochemical reactions of certain multicellular architectures. Nevertheless, as enduring as it is, this belief has undergone a clear regression since the 14th century when horses, pigs, and dogs were prosecuted in court, judged, condemned and executed on par with the responsibility—thus freedom—presumed of humans. And since Ribot, with the exception of developmental disability, it has become well established that all behavior, even among humans, is fully determined, though the mechanism of such determination often remains obscure in its details.[12] Free will, this immediate datum of consciousness, is no more true than the fixity of the Earth or the parallelism of vertical lines which, although slightly less immediate, are also data of consciousness.[13] A religious, social and political imposture, the illusion of free will nonetheless possesses, as do all ghosts, a functional reality—a component of the soul which Malebranche considered a mere function.[14]

The Confusion of Categories

Chance, determinism, and freedom shift from a status of truth to that of a lie according to the dimensions of the phenomenon we observe. Therefore they do not constitute, as we are wont to believe, fixed and categorically opposed systems, but relative ones, with floating aspects, poorly differentiated among themselves, constantly overstepping each other, merging, overlapping and intermingling, like clouds. No hiker who, at dawn or dusk, admires the transfigurations of a mountain landscape is naive enough to believe there are twenty kinds of snow: violet, orange, blue, pink. On the contrary, he keeps a firm belief in the existence of a typically white snow. Still, snow is in itself no more white than colored, or even black. More credulous than the alpine tourist is the amateur who, in laboratories and libraries, tries his hand at philosophical-scientific tourism, from the atom to the galaxy, the mineral to the human, or the social, and becomes convinced of the existence of as many perfectly distinct types of reality as there are viewpoints and distances in space and time from which phenomena may be considered: here they are material and random, there they are spiritual and free. Such qualifications aspire to be irreducible, yet they are but a shimmer of changing reflections.

The Wrong Side
Equals the Right Side

Relationship of Cause and Effect or
a Simple Relation of Succession?

From another point of view, the cinematograph invites us to reconsider the principle of causality.

Recorded or projected in reverse motion, a movie shows the birth of slight condensations in limpid air. Progressively, these thicken and gather in swirls that, slowly becoming heavier, lower into the mouth of a firearm out of which, resulting from this proximity, a flame suddenly erupts. In such a mode of representation smoke precedes fire, and if we hesitate to assert that smoke induces fire, it is only because we are more used to the opposite mode of representation, which science has had time to festoon with a thousand justifications. Yet, if we were accustomed to more often seeing fire succeeding smoke, we would become inclined to think that smoke is the cause of fire and that there exists, from smoke to fire, a mysterious force-link, an intractable determining influence, an essential necessity, as we believe so firmly is the case in the other direction, from fire to smoke.

The Uselessness of Causes?

In a fragment of the strange universe that a movie in reverse motion displays, we have no problem squashing the emerging fancy of an absurd causality through criticism: it is only the result of a relation of succession that was arbitrarily introduced. But you can replay the same movie as many times as you want, this same relation will always remain and takes the figure of a law, statistically established, about a little world, in the same way the laws of ours are established. Within the particular structure of cinematographic continuity in reverse motion—a structure that seems odd only because it is exceptional, but on second thought is no more striking than the space-time structures averred at terrestrial, subatomic or universal scales—we must agree that everything takes place as if smoke was the cause of fire. Indeed, within continuity, which today we hold as most real, scientists and philosophers do not dare affirm the opposite relation in a more categorical way: that everything takes place as if fire was the cause of smoke. Causality appears to be little more than a mental coloration bestowed upon certain degrees of probability within a succession of phenomena, about which it is entirely indifferent, and often impossible, to know whether, they are independent of or dependent on each other in another way.

Because it is so obvious in the anti-universe moving on screen, the uselessness of the causal relationship is thereby revealed more clearly within the natural order of things, in which this relationship is a mere specter created by the mind. If there are causes, they are useless. We must then recognize that nature can do away with them, for it is everywhere faithful to one of its most general principles: that of minimal action. We must therefore presume the universe to be devoid of all laws other than those of pure numbers, that is, frightfully simple and scandalously monotonous laws hiding beneath the vertiginous and shaky ideologies in which the human mind wraps itself.

The Absurdity of Causes

Then again, what would a cause be, for instance, this primordial cause: gravity and universal attraction? A virtue, a power, nothing that is material, a kind of spirit? And how would this spirit exert its mysterious power on objects? We would smirk at those who claim that the Earth hypnotizes the Moon to enslave it in a circular motion. Still, this is no less extravagant or obscure a proposition than pretending that the terrestrial mass communicates its weight to a stone and forces it to fall. All in all, a greater effort of faith and fancy is required to believe in a world of causes than to admit the viability of a gratuitous world.

Long ago, when doubt arose as to whether Providence was good or at least just, a thousand reasons were discovered to exonerate God of human ills. Innocents about to be hanged for murders they had not committed would recall in their last moments that they had neglected for three years to recite their paternoster, succeeding thereby in legitimating their unjust punishment in their own conscience, through a cause respecting the logic of theologians. Today, we dare to think that the supposed Creator cares not for justice and goodness, yet we gladly picture him as an infallible engineer incapable of making errors of calculation. Hence, just as soon as a new comet appears in the sky, we hurriedly attribute a whole collection of exact mechanical determinations to it. But perhaps soon we will feel that the universe no more resembles the work of a genius mechanic than that of the Holy of Holies—that it resembles nothing.

Gratuitous Ends

If there are no causes, there can be no effects, or ends, even less final ends than original ones. Indeed, while causality still remains a rather general article of faith, for a long time finality has seemed conjectural and illusory to most. To believe in causes while doubting their ends makes for a rather wobbly mindset, albeit one which is widespread today. Through this wobbliness, the weakening of the causal category, which is progressively declining, has become more manifest.

However, the very same people who deride the famous melon slices to which Bernardin de Saint-Pierre assigned, as a preconceived end, the joy of being easily divided among the appetites of a familial table, will also seriously claim that the development of plants, as consumers of CO_2 and fixatives for nitrogen, was necessitated, according to the plan of creation, by the breathing requirements of animal species that henceforth multiplied. Reasoning with the same egocentric formula, these same people would argue that the chestnuts of the Champs-Elysées always required, for their growth and the exercise of their chlorophyll functions, the swarming of the human species, creators of civilization and urbanism as well as producers of CO_2.

A Cause That Is an End
or an End That Is a Cause

Ultimately, can we imagine a more absurd sequence with a more arbitrary finalism than this: a whole city with its neighborhoods, streets and buildings was conceived only to allow the doorbell to ring at a given flat? Yet, this is a rather common dream: the sleeper knows, without knowing why, that it is requisite for him to hurry through the hardships and traffic dangers of an immense city. At long last, he arrives before a building and suddenly understands it was his destination. He flies up tall and long stairs, reaching tangled hallways that further delay the traveler, now rife with anxiety—until they agree to let him pass, leading him to a door where he merely has to ring the bell. The ringing triggers his awakening to the sound of an alarm clock that went off a few seconds ago within the other reality to which he has returned. This gap—very small in waking time but very long in sleeping time—was necessary to allow the hearing stimulus to break through the thickness of sleep and reach consciousness. But it was enough to let the nervous impulse, as it traveled, generate and orient a series of dream images aimed at justifying, in the logic of dreaming, the auditory sensation already received by the neurons but not yet clearly perceived.

We should note here that the most implausible finalism appears perfectly true: the ringing of the alarm-clock is at once the end and the cause, the predetermined end and the posterior cause, from which the series of dreamed events starts and where it leads, that is to say, in a certain way, of lived events as well. Dreams, we might argue, are but a play of mad thoughts. However, except perhaps during the instant of extreme pain or total physical pleasure, what do we know outside of thought? As for judging whether here thought is sane and there insane, it is merely a matter of personal appreciation varying from person to person and, in the same individual, from moment to moment. For many a revered mystic, illustrious philosopher or great poet, the tenuous logic of exterior life indeed bore less truth than the harmonious and fecund madness of their dreams. In our extrovert civilization, our organism is generally unable to attend as much to the facts of sleep as to those of wakefulness. Nonetheless, all those who have endeavored for some time to recover the memory of their dreams know how easily such memory can be educated to the point of becoming cumbersome. Hence the habit that accords an equal importance to both modes of thought can grow quickly. In fact, does not the most active person often find himself absorbed in reflections foreign to his actions, behaving for a few minutes like a sleepwalker? We would therefore be ill-advised to deny any value to finality under the pretext that it manifests itself all too clearly in the course of dreaming.

Logical Inversion or Logical Straightening

In a more precise way, we should also notice, in the alarm-clock dream, that the cause was transformed into an effect as a consequence of a transplant into time. During the few seconds of external time when, as the sensation was inhibited, that is, delayed in its transmission to the sleeper's consciousness, the nervous impulse nonetheless acted on and directed his mental life. Its very quick rhythm—or inner time—subsequently triggered the development of a long association of images that depicted a length of several hours tending to facilitate the advent of the sensation into clear perception, according to the architectural rules of the dream. Sound, as cause in outer time, became an end in inner time, based on the difference of value of both times. A slight delay in perception in a slowed down time, lengthily exploited by imagination in a precipitated time—these are the conditions of a complete inversion of determinism, a half-rotation in what we might call logical space: one end for the other, finality for beginning, effect for cause.

We do know of another—absolutely general—instance of psycho-physiological acrobatics: the realignment of retinal images. Yet these words, realignment and inversion, merely signify habits of seeing and judging things, and for the sake of simplicity, most of the time one way rather than another. If our retinal images weren't realigned in correlation with the data from other senses, we would likely have gotten used to a more complex coordination of movements, as well as a better understanding of the equivalence of top and bottom. For there is no absolute top or bottom, since we are all on Earth at the antipode of others, each with our particular little tops and bottoms. Similarly, there is no right or wrong side, past or future, cause or finality. Like geometric space, the space of time and that of logic always comprise an antipode: they are themselves and their opposite, depending on their function in each instant and each place. That is what we might ponder when we watch the unusual unfolding of a movie where the plow pulls the oxen and smoke falls into the chimney.

Photo-Electric Psychoanalysis

Inside as Outside, Everything Is but Poetry

Long before the use of the cinematograph, it was certainly well-known that "everything appears yellow to whomever is jaundiced" as Lucretius noted, that "the world is but abuse," as Villon complained, and that "A Thousand and One Nights govern the world," as Voltaire mused.[15] Still, a few reflections inspired by the cinematograph might better contribute to demonstrating the inconsistency of the last notions still generally held to be quasi-certain truths, the permanent foundations of knowledge. Hence, today, the reality of space and time, determinism and freedom, matter and spirit, or the universe's continuity and discontinuity loses its contours, its consistency, its necessity, and tends to become a conditional, floating, allegorical, and intermittent reality: all in all, it becomes poetry.

If we are slowly learning, and without too many regrets, that all we can know of the outside world is an arrangement of more or less useful fables, as soon as it is a matter of self-examination, humans—who have always had a high idea of themselves—stubbornly refuse to reconsider who they are. Surely, this impregnable veneration of the self is necessary to endure, that is to say, to mask the vile aspects of living. And the Socratic precept, though unrealizable in full, may be dangerous to follow for the legions who would sink into self-disgust and self-loathing if, in getting to know themselves slightly less poorly, they lacked the courage to accept what they saw. Happy are the weak-minded, the complete extroverts, all muscle, instinct and action, who know not to know themselves! But the rest, the majority among the civilized, are not so obtuse that they don't suffer from this more or less acute conflict, the sources of all psychoses: needing to imagine themselves, thus to know themselves, at the same time as they refuse to accept themselves as soon as their deeper personality is laid bare.

The Machine for the Confession of Souls

The horror, or at the very least the embarrassment, that a filmed individual feels in front of his animated image, leads us to suspect that it publicized something of the personal secret which the subject forced himself not to know. All the little people, the hunchbacks, the pockmarked, and the obese, long accustomed to their reflection in mirrors inverted right-to-left, see themselves as less ungraceful than nature made them; all humans, in the labor of their imagination, judge themselves to be less cowardly and two-faced—almost as honest, handsome, and intelligent or distinguished as can be.[16] The cinematographic lens displays no such complacency. What viewers notice first in their on screen double is the vulgarity of their attitude, the awkwardness of their gesture, or this shame in their eyes that they had so endeavored, successfully they thought, in concealing. But the ghost speaks as well, in a voice that the living, in all sincerity, do not and cannot recognize, because they have never heard it from the outside before, born by another breath than his or her own. The microphone and the loud-speaker transmit accents of an unbearable immodesty, disclosing the naiveté of false pride, the bitterness of denied failures, the worry underneath assurance and laughter—all the weakness and deceit of a character thinking itself straight, weathered, and victorious over itself. Few are the confessors capable of seeing and listening as deep into the soul as the glassy gaze of the photoelectric ear!

Fortunately for him, very quickly after the third or fourth projection, the viewer and listener of his own distress, regaining his self-control, will be absolved again: he will have corrected himself, renewing the lies of his impressions, healing the most caustic of his flayed wounds.

A Clairvoyance That Can Help Justice

Certainly, the speaking image of a person doesn't reveal his truth. However, if we gauge the reaction of filmed subjects—who scratch where it itches—we must recognize that the lucidities of the screen present a psychological transect of its characters at the level of the slightest lie as well as purest sincerity. American courts have already taken stock of, and legally used, this inquisitive power of the cinematograph, particularly for ascertaining maternal rights by observing the reactions of infants placed, suddenly and successively, before two women claiming to be their mother.

This process would provide finer and more reliable results if cinematographic slow motion was employed (as long as it was a viable slow motion that would not extinguish expression). Studied in close up, through image and sound, mimicry and voice, an interrogation would reveal many jolts of surprise, defensive clenchings, worries, hesitations, and anxieties of the accused, or, on the contrary, would show the disbelief, the assurance, the faultless indignation of a subject of good faith wrongly suspected. Of course, all this would not go without the possibility of error, and yet, with many more chances to see justice, it also has the advantage of avoiding having to resort to brutality for confession.[17]

From the Sacrament of Penitence to Psychoanalysis

It is not only for justice that psychological scrutiny through the cinematograph might be useful. For a long time now, humans have vaguely felt their anxieties, from a simple scruple to downright psychosis—anxieties they suffer when the pleasing idea they made and want to retain of themselves doesn't succeed in sufficiently repressing the revelations of a looming stranger self who is contemptible, threatening, and monstrous—are diminished or appeased by the confession of this angst, and of its cause, through its exteriorization in speech, through its rejection, then, outside the inner world. This relief is confirmed by the adage, "an offense admitted is half forgiven," and it explains why Catholicism instituted the sacrament of penitence as an outlet for the venomous fermentations of the mind. Although with brilliance, Freud did nothing more when perfecting this therapy into psychoanalysis.[18]

In the areas of education and therapy, the cinematograph, especially through slow motion, offers the means of a sound introduction to psychoanalysis, with a useful detection, not so much for the truly disturbed as for the large crowds of paranormals, many of whom are capable of becoming acquainted with their imbalance and understanding their behavioral problems in order to get them in check or correct them to a large extent.

Knowing Ourselves Better, in Order to Better Lie to Ourselves

If typical and irremediable anomalies remain exceptions, nonetheless there exists a quasi-majority, a great number of half-worried subjects, intermittently anxious, grossly ashamed, or very shy, whose slight imbalance might be amended to the extent that the source of their problem may be brought to their consciousness. That is where the slow motion of both the cinematograph and sound should be able to render great services to an attentive and patient observer.

More generally, the cinematographic analysis is usable for what we may call lessons in upkeep that are extremely necessary for many professions and social conditions. Hence, public figures, officials, orators, lawyers, celebrities, even small business owners or individuals concerned with a good appearance—that is to say, everyone—would greatly benefit from seeing themselves on screen over and over, listening to themselves like actors do, progressively correcting their imperfections, perfecting their role, and learning to lie through it in an entirely convincing way. In this case, the cinematograph uncovers disagreeable truths only for the purpose of squashing them: this apparatus of sincerity is just as much a school of lies.

Mechanical Philosophy

The Psychology of Machines

A driver who knows his car well speaks of it with the same terms a rider uses to speak of his horse. He calls it docile or reticent, soft or responsive, supple and reliable, or stubborn and touchy. He knows the best way to handle it to derive the maximum of efforts from it: at times he uses gentleness, at other times roughness; sometimes he gives it a rest, or lets it go and pushes it to the utmost, from the beginning to the end of a run. Two engines of the same brand and same series are rarely the same: each displays its own character through the particulars of its behavior. This is because the complexity of the inner structure and interactions of a mechanical organism leads to the individualization of the machine and impels, with regard to its overall working, a tinge of unpredictability which signals the very beginning of what we call, at varying degrees of development, freedom, will, or soul.

Depending on their complexity and subtlety, all instruments that require the attentive care of humans, so as to ensure their optimal use, acquire from this attention, albeit implicitly, certain psychological characteristics. And, as anyone can attest, it is a fact that a fountain pen becomes used to a certain penmanship with such attunement that it will not allow variation; a watch that faithfully kept time for twenty years in the father's pocket will stop working in a few days when handed down to his son, mindful as he may be, for even the watchmaker cannot restore the personal climate in which the mechanism has become accustomed to live.

Whether Mechanical or Organic, the Complexity of an Apparatus Creates Its Own Psychic Aspect

A cell is certainly a being, but a soul emerges only through a colony of cells, all the more clearly when the colony is constituted of numerous and better-differentiated elements within a cooperative whole of a higher organization. A spring, a cog, or a valve are only die-cast metal, but a community of gears and pistons, functionally assembled, displays tendencies, habits and whims that form a rudiment of mind—and this psychological aspect is all the more apparent when the mechanism has a complex structure and complex functions. At a certain degree of multiplicity and architectural and functional sophistication, machines routinely behave in such a way that humans, against their better judgment, must recognize a kind of habituation in them. It amounts to a convergence of sensibility and memory, and also implies some kind of choice and discernment about proper and improper working, that is to say, between good and evil, as well as some latitude, some fantasy—a trace of freedom by the system in response to the forces we impress upon it and within it. Hence the fundamental observation of Ribot who underlined the fact that the psyche emerges through the growth of the number of possible reactions among multiple nervous components, may be transposed into the inorganic world where it applies to the interplay of mechanical elements.

Linked to the Functioning of a Whole
That We Cannot Easily Locate,
the Spiritual Character is Foremost Ubiquitous

Seeking to recognize the slightest bit of spirit in a farm tractor might seem excessive. But, to begin with, what is spirit? We generally only agree upon what it seems not to be: it couldn't be material because we cannot exactly situate its insertion points in matter, nor can we fathom how it communicates with and commands matter. A good part of the human soul has been assigned residence in the brain, yet the heart, kidneys, liver, gallbladder and other still more mysterious organs have also claimed the honor of housing our invisible spirituality. The soul is everywhere in humans, and nowhere in particular. It results from the whole of organic function. Similarly, the personal character of a motor does not dwell exclusively in this or that part: carburetor or magneto, piston or cylinder head. This character is also an impalpable being, a global product of the activity of all mechanical organs.[19]

Much simpler figures also possess a characteristic aspect that we cannot connect to any of their parts, but to which the collaboration of all these parts is indispensable. Hence the essential virtue of a Euclidian triangle is that the sum of its angles equals two right angles. Where does the character of this species come from? Neither from one angle nor the other, nor from its sides or heights or surface: it is everywhere and nowhere, it is a spirit.

Beyond the Spirituality Common
to All Superior Machines, the
Cinematograph Develops Its Own Genius

Like any mechanism, and proportionally to its own degree of complexity, the cinematographic apparatus—in its multiplicity, comprising both camera and projector, sound recording and reproduction devices, and all their assemblies—possesses this personality that characterizes all superior objects, though in this case it might appear diffuse on account of the different contraptions through which it is implemented: thus it represents the collective personality of a small society of machines. However, beyond these characters of first individualization, a usual occurrence in the world of machines, the cinematograph displays its own genius loud and clear, of which no other mechanism has until now given such a pointed example.

Other systems born of the human mind, especially optical ones, have certainly reacted to it for a long time, allowing the human mind to reform and considerably develop its theories of the universe. Copernicus, Galileo, Kepler, Newton and Laplace were trained to rethink the world according to the images their astronomical telescopes delivered to them from the sky, in the same way that Spallanzani, Claude Bernard, and Pasteur were led to build or rebuild anatomy, physiology and pathology in accordance with the particular vision of their magnifying glasses and microscopes. Still, these enlarging lenses only multiply and transform—exclusively visual—uni-sensorial data that address only one category of the mind, optical extent [*étendue*]. Hence the modifications that these instruments propose to philosophical and scientific conceptions can only present themselves to intelligence by way of the spatial category in the same way as ordinary messages from a single sense, however important it may be: sight. For the researcher or the philosopher, a telescope can do nothing more than amplify the work of the external perception of an organ—an artificial super-eye that sees farther or closer or deeper, but does nothing else but look, unable as it is to mechanically combine data belonging to several rational categories. In other words, it cannot think.

The cinematograph differs from solely optical apparatuses firstly in that it gathers information pertaining to two distinct senses from the outside world, and secondly and foremost, in that, in and of itself, it presents this bisensorial data as arranged into specific rhythms of succession. The cinematograph is a witness that recounts a figure of sensible reality that is not only spatial but temporal, integrating its representations into an architecture whose relief presupposes the synthesis of two intellectual categories (extension and duration), a synthesis in which a third category emerges almost automatically: causation. Through this power of effecting diverse combinations, the cinematograph, though it may be purely mechanical, proves to be more than an instrument of enlargement or replacement for one or several of the sense organs. Through this power, which is one of the fundamental characteristics of any intellectual activity among living beings, the cinematograph stands out as a substitute and annex of the organ in which the faculty that coordinates perceptions is generally located—the brain—the alleged center of intelligence.

No, the thinking machine is not exactly a utopia any longer; the cinematograph, like the computing machine, represents its first implementation, already working far better than a rough model. Leibniz, who obtained the notes and drafts left by Pascal, succeeded in working out the cog system that the Jansenist mathematician had invented without being able to make it function properly. Since then, evermore perfected, a purely mechanical device knows how to group the numbers it is provided in accordance with the fundamental algorithms of mathematics, not exactly in the same way the human mind does, but better, since it is errorless. Yet—one might object—this machine does not think. Then what is it actually doing when its work replaces the cerebral task of the calculator to perfection? We should recognize that a mechanical thinking exists alongside organic thought, and while it resembles organic thinking, we are only beginning to learn to activate this mechanical thinking that will expand in future robots and whose implementation is logically prescribed by the development of our civilization. This mechanical pre-thought would seem to be unconscious: but this presents an objection neither to its existence nor to its affiliation with the human soul, since today we agree that the latter is largely unknown to itself.[20]

The Philosophy of the Cinematograph

The cinematograph is among the still partially intellectual robots that, with two photo and electro-mechanical senses, as well as a photochemical recording memory, shapes representations—that is, thought—in which we discern the primordial framework of reason: the three categories of extension, duration, and causation. This would already be a remarkable result if cinematographic thought, as in the case of the calculating machine, were only mimicking human ideation. On the contrary, we know that the cinematograph inscribes its own character within its representations of the universe with such originality that it makes this representation not simply a record or copy of the conceptions of its organic mastermind [*mentalité-mère*], but indeed a differently individualized system, partly independent, comprising the seed of the development of a philosophy that strays far enough from common opinions so as to be called an antiphilosophy.

Quantity
Mother of Quality[21]

Indivisibility of Space-Time

The fundamental difference between the intellectual human mechanism and the cinematographic mechanism of capture and expression consists in the fact that in the former the notions of space and time can exist separately—and a certain effort is even needed to conceive of their perennial union—while in the latter any representation of space is automatically adjoined to its time value, which is to say that it cannot conceive of space outside of its movement in time. Hence, humans may keep the image of an attitude or the memory of something said present in mind for several seconds or more, so long as their attention will not waiver, but without concern for this duration, indeed as though it did not exist. By contrast, the cinematograph can only provide such an image or sound within the body of a temporal rhythm, ordinarily set at twenty-two to twenty-three frames per second. In human understanding, there is space and there is time, whence, painstakingly, results the synthesis of space-time. In cinematographic understanding, there is only space-time.

Absolute Relativism

We know that this cinematographic time is essentially variable, while the rhythm of time, as humans usually perceive it, is, on the contrary, constant: this is another difference between the intellect of the living being and that of the mechanical being, and it is to the credit of the latter. In contrast to fixed space and invariable time, typically considered independent of each other and which form the two classical primordial categories of human understanding, is space-time, always mobile and changing, a singular framework within which the cinematograph inscribes its representations.

The variability of cinematographic time and its interdependence with space lead, as we have seen, to constant transformations correlative to all semblances located in this four-dimensional continuum. This more than general relativity translates into the breaking up and intermingling of all classifications that seemed fundamental and immutable within the extra-cinematographic universe. Depending on the different temporary values assumed by the dimensions of space-time, discontinuity may become continuous and continuity discontinuous; rest can produce movement and movement rest; matter can acquire or lose spirit; the inert can become alive and the living dead-like; randomness can become determinate or sever its causes; finalities can mutate into origins; and evident truths can turn into absurdities immediately perceived as such.

These changes of quality—of primordial qualities in fact—are subject to variations in the duration and magnitude of the objects observed, in relation to reference values belonging to the world closest to the observing subject and thus at the human scale. Quality is therefore a function of measure and number. Quality devolves from quantity. Quantity and quality become correlative and interchangeable notions that merge into one another to form a quantity-quality continuum as a covariant of space-time. Hence, the philosophy of the cinematograph fuses the second and third attributes of Aristotle.[22]

Quantity is the Agent
of Any Qualitative Transmutation

With his very first math lessons, a child learns that by adding apples to apples he will always get a sum of apples, and that quantitative arithmetic operations change nothing in the quality of the objects added or multiplied, subtracted or divided. Yet this principle is false. Ten trees added together makes a clump, a thousand makes a grove, and ten thousand a forest. A forest possesses many attributes of which each of its trees is ignorant. A grain of sand is what it is; billions of grains of sand cannot be imagined as grains: they have become a desert, the Sahara, the land of thirst and mirages. A trace of musk is a perfume, a gram of it is a stench. One dollar is a hundred cents, but twenty millions dollars cannot be thought in terms of cents; moreover, these are not dollars anymore but a fortune: luxury, elegance, leisure and happiness. A few neurons trigger a reflex arc; a thousand reflex arcs become a character, an intelligence, a soul. A crowd is something quite different from several hundred individuals: it is endowed with a sensibility, a will and a freedom very distinct from the individual wills, sensibilities and freedoms of which it is made up, and forms a monstrous, unreasonable, versatile, childish and savage being. In music, a minute has three thousand six hundred thirds; but a century—that of Pericles or Louis the Fourteenth—what possible relation could it have in our mind with all the thirds adding up to it? It is a sensory truth in all cases that, except for very small differences, a variation in quantity in the same objects occasions a variation in the quality of the whole. An increase or decrease in number in itself brings about new qualities.

The deep equivalences of quantity and quality revealed by the cinematograph alter classical systemization in its basic principle: they usher in the fundamental unity of all forms within the universal relativity of all species, and all types of objects and beings. To be sure, number was held to be a kind of general quality apart from others, qualifying secondarily, as it were, each of the qualities themselves. Yet on screen, number shows that it controls the power of qualification entirely and on its own, and that through the interplay of increases and decreases it is the unique quality of all that exists in perception.

Auguste Comte warned us not to infer the multiple out of the simple, for in doing so we risk transgressing specific boundaries and, from quantity to quantity, finding ourselves in a realm of differing quality and foreign laws. We don't know exactly where, or when, or how inorganic elements, by adding themselves to others, become a semi-living, organic molecule in the protein of a virus. Nor do we know the precise conditions and limits under which neurons associating with one another accumulate enough interactions for instinct and intelligence to emerge. Yet these mysterious transmutations harbor a terrible simplicity: they are a function of number. In the same way, it is a temporal number, the quantity of movement in time, that governs the transmutations of slow and accelerated motion in the cinematographic universe.

Humans: The Only Quantitative
Standard in the Universe

If any differentiation only has a quantitative meaning for all things at their core, then it is the order of magnitude of phenomena that remains, in the end, the sole foundation of the distinction, classification and knowledge we build upon them. Depending on its dimensions, an object, being, or event is located in this or that qualitative zone of space, time, and logic. In effect, space is flat or curved, matter is continuous or discontinuous, mechanics is determined or random, laws are causal or probabilistic, only in relation to the scale at which we study them: the average, or the infinitely small or big.

Yet this immensity, or middle ground, or tininess of things, upon which their qualities are dependent, is gauged in comparison to humans and always will be. It is human measure and the dimensions immediately available to it that constitute the standards according to which we evaluate any magnitude, number or quantity. It is only the distance at which a phenomenon appears that renders it small or large and determines the spatial, temporal and logical properties of that province of the universe in which it occurs. Hence, the total relativity of all the aspects of nature has for its only hinge, reference, and sovereign judge, humanity; that is to say, the height, weight, and shape of humans, the length of their limbs, and the reach of their sight and hearing.

All our systems of knowledge, all our science and philosophy, all our certainties and doubts, all our truths and eternal unknowns are closely adjusted to this average altitude of five feet and a few inches at which our brow overhangs the ground. We might doubt whether a smaller nose on Cleopatra might have changed the face of the world, since love doesn't always concern beauty, but certainly other theodicies and cosmogonies, and different mathematics and logic would have resulted from a human species the size of a bacterium or the Himalayas.

That all constructions of thought acknowledge as their ultimate criterion nothing more than the human dimension, whose episodic and precarious character we intuit better than anything else, demonstrates to a scandalous degree the vanity of our pretentions and the powerlessness of our need to take hold of some fulcrum outside of ourselves, some scrap of unconditional certainty, or the slightest hint of the existence of some fixed value. All the efforts intelligence makes to escape from its relative condition are as painfully vain and absurd as someone trying to pull himself up out of quicksand by his own hair. Humanity is the only measure of the universe, yet this measure measures itself according to what it seeks to measure: it is relative among relative measures—an absolute variable.

The Relativity of Logic

The Incredible Reversibility of Time

Time's reversibility, the possibility of which we witness in the universe represented by the cinematograph, constitutes another capital difference with the properties of our everyday universe. Within our mental life, this reversibility shows up so rarely and remains so totally foreign to our external experiences that it remains completely incredible. It seems to be a pure play of the machine, an artifice devoid of any real meaning, and even endowed with a comical character contrasting with the invariable order of successions we experience everywhere else. Nonetheless, whether we like it or not, temporal reversibility occurs in cinematographic representation with a constancy that makes it a law of this system—as sure as any law can be. We struggle to conceive of the fact that rigorous principles of identity and causality cease to be applicable in the world of the atom, yet we defer to the physicists' arguments, however subtle their theories may be. Conversely, although the cinematograph gives us visual proof of the ambivalent order in which phenomena succeed each other on screen, and with a much greater force of evidence, in spite of the fact that we know that world much better and more closely than that of the atom, we are reluctant to grant the reversibility of filmed action the slightest bit of attention.

That's because the cinematographic world—as it is said contemptuously—is but a fictive world.

The Legitimacy of Fiction

Fictive, however, means neither false nor non-existing. No one would deny the fact that the work of the imagination is usable in practice. "Everything one invents is true," Flaubert asserted. Even if everything we invented was not true, it would become so. Today, most psychologists and psychiatrists, whether proponents or opponents of Freud, recognize in the imaginary world par excellence—that of dreaming—a psychological truth that is superior to that of extroverted, rationalized and presumably objective thought. Indeed, the personality of the sleeper, freed from the majority of logical and moral constraints of exterior life, can manifest itself more freely and reveal more of its intimate nature in dream images.

The Cinematograph: A Dreaming Machine

The processes employed by the dream discourse, and which facilitate its deep sincerity, find an analogue in cinematographic style.

We might start with the use of synecdoches, in which a part stands for the whole, or a meaningless and banal detail is enlarged and repeated so as to become the center and leitmotiv of a whole scene, whether dreamed or seen on screen. It might be a key or a knotted ribbon in a woman's hair or a telephone, which the dream and the screen both show in close up, charged with an immense emotional force or the full dramatic signification accorded to that object when it was first noted during our waking life or at the beginning of the movie.

Moreover, and consequently, in the language of dreams as in that of the cinematograph, these word-images undergo a transposition of meaning, a symbolization. It is no longer a matter of a key, knotted ribbon, or telephone. The key would be more accurately translated as "Will I muster the courage to commit this indiscretion that will allow me to put my mind at ease?" and the knotted ribbon means "But she loved me!" and the telephone, "By now he must be out of danger." In truth, and in truth of fact, such signs are magical formulas summarizing a whole universe of lived, living and yet-to-be-lived impressions that no verbal expression could faithfully translate in their entirety.

Finally, dream action, proceeds like action on film, each within their own eventful ad lib temporality, in which simultaneities may be drawn out into successions, or successions compressed into coincidences, and whose difference with external time may lead to effects of inversion.

Prejudice Against the Dream of the Apparatus

The enlargement and metaphorization of details, the heightening and transformation of the signifying value of such symbols, the particularity of time—all such analogies between dream language and the language of the cinematograph should lead us to the conclusion that the latter, like the former, is constitutionally inclined to express truths with great psychological faithfulness, profoundly exact from the purview of the figuration of mental life.

Yet, on the contrary, this may be what causes or reinforces the general diffidence we witness toward the philosophical relevance of cinematographic images. For while the completely introverted dream-life is infinitely richer in sincerity and feeling, and thus richer in poetry, it is considered to be dangerous, cursed and inferior to the mental life of wakefulness, which is nothing more than a vulgar extroverted schematization of the former.

Realism of Introverted Thought and Idealism of Extroverted Thought

The prohibition against introversion is likely due to the fact that dreams not only appear to contribute nothing directly to the conservation of the individual or the species, but also go against this instinct. To be sure, this is a rather narrow-minded purview. Is not to despise, fear, and counter introverted thought in order to cultivate and exalt extroversion akin to trying to obtain light and warmth without fire, or metal without ore, or fruits without fruit trees? What is extroverted thought if not the result of the maturation and crystallization of introverted thought into more abstract, select and organized forms in order to adapt to outer appearances? Extroverted thought is a second degree thought, a thought about thoughts, an imagination born of imaginations, a dream begotten by dreams, and in this sense it is not less but more subjective, as we can easily observe in certain scaffoldings of genuinely scientific theories. Is the electron's spin or the curvature of space objective? Are love and hatred, symbolized by a knotted ribbon, subjective? Yes, certainly, but they are profoundly real.

Notions of a flat and immobile Earth corresponding to simple realities of daily experience, have given way to the notions of terrestrial sphericity and rotation, followed by those of the movement of the solar system, then those of the receding of stars, the expansion and contraction of the universe, etc., which increasingly prove to be nothing more than ideas straying ever farther from the objectivity they invoke. Science, which claims to be the extroverted mode of knowledge par excellence, is evolving against its own claim in the direction of more abstraction, that is to say, increased introversion. Its extreme rationalization transforms it into a mathematical dream that has infinitely more distant relations with human reality—the only somewhat real reality—than the most incoherent nightmares.

The human mind is endowed with a rather restricted faculty of extroversion, placed between two much more extended realms of introversion: one in which introversion figures as the original form of all thought, the immediate spectacle of the ego, and the source of first truths drawn from an undeniable subjectivity; the other in which introversion presents itself as the most elaborate mode of thought, beyond the intermediary mode of extroversion, whose abstractions, although intended for outer use, are taken up and treated almost exclusively according to reasonable ideation that is inured to the contradictions that might result, whether with externally sensible, hence objective, data, or with the data from the inner sense, that is, from original introspection. In finally being introverted to the utmost degree, reason speculates through a subjectivity that dares not speak its name, that is as devoid as possible of sentimental confirmation and individual authenticity, and is reduced to a dry geometric fantasy, like the images in a kaleidoscope's mirror that correspond to nothing true or alive.

Since all humans are at once the principal object and the sole agent of knowledge, it goes without saying that true objectivity—to the extent there can be such a thing—is to be found in the subject's most direct apprehension of his own existence: in the original introversion that occurs in dream and daydream analysis. In other words, in the purest form of subjectivity least clouded and constrained by exterior influences. While, of course, extroverted thought has its use and its truth, it is nonetheless far from having a monopoly on such virtues. Although in practice introverted thought is insufficient by itself, it does not deserve the lack of consideration and diffidence with which certain people treat it, hoping to paint with the same brush all that proceeds from these cinematographic images akin to dream language.

Causal Orientation in Space-Time

We must therefore take the inversion of the course of time as a truth, and the necessary examples are provided by the cinematograph and dreams: the inner reality of the world of dreams and of the screen. This reversibility affects the intuition of the relations of cause and effect at its core, for the mind refuses to accept that events, whose order of succession may be reversed, are linked by some necessary causality. The principle of causality ceases to appear absolutely valid and becomes a correlate of the vectorial direction of the fourth dimension of space: time. Depending upon its temporal orientation in space, a phenomenon can be either cause or effect. And when this orientation changes, we observe the substitution of the causal function for the effect function, and vice versa.

Since causality proves to also be a covariant of time, the space-time continuum would seem to be endowed with a logical character, and the relativity of space and time includes the relativity of logic. Every space has its own logical orientation determined by the direction of its movement in time. Causality is a spatial and temporal function representing the fifth variable of the continuum we are most used to conceptualizing.

Over-Determination Through the Multiplicity of Time

In considering causality as a temporal function, we can better understand the over-determination that characterizes certain dreams in which events present themselves with several causes, each being judged as necessary and sufficient in itself. Indeed, a dream sometimes constructs a particularly intricate universe because it is multi-temporal. Peripheral excitations in the present, as well as memories of previously lived impressions of experiences, make their way from the unconscious to consciousness with very uneven speeds, and according to their very different qualities. Each of these elements inserts itself with its own temporality within the dream synthesis, which it tries to direct for its own benefit. These various times bring their particular causalities with them and are totalizing, that is to say that the events in each time occur at a precisely determined place in their order of succession. Hence when two or several components coincide and add up their effects into a dream image, that image, because it is located at the intersection of two or more times, finds itself fully determined by the causal function of each time at once.

Indetermination Through Deficient Time

Conversely, an indetermination leads us to assume it might be linked to some failure or irregularity of the time-value. But as of now we know of only one instance of randomness that could be true: Heisenberg's formulas describe the unique uncertainty that depicts not the statistical expression of the effect of an excess of microscopic determinants, but the result of a fundamental incompatibility between two partial determinants that exclude each other, while their coexistence would be required for a complete determination. In this case, calculus is able to precisely locate a corpuscle in space, yet unable to provide its quantity of movement, that is, its existence value in relation to time; or conversely, when calculus indicates its exact time-value, it can no longer express its space-value. It then appears that, in the universe that we encounter at the subatomic scale, the spatial framework is mathematically disconnected from its temporal orientation. With the unity of space-time thus severed, phenomena manifest themselves under the guise of lesser determination and lesser reality, in a logical penumbra as it were, more or less defined either through optical extent [*étendue*] or time, but never under the full and sure light of these two notions conjoined to the maximum of their enlightening power. In the very proportion through which they become independent of the temporal dimension, the three spatial dimensions reveal themselves insufficient for properly framing the chains of cause and effect. By separating itself from space, time robs space of the causality it had brought into it.

Even Plane Geometry is a Geometry in Time

However, rather than closely linking causality to time, would it not be more fitting to consider it a joint estate between space and time, inherent not to any of the four dimensions of the continuum, but born of their synthesis? Such a position is perfectly defensible in a domain that admits several outward appearances of truth, none of which can claim to entirely exclude the others.

Indeed, the mind cannot conceive of an experimental framework in which space and time might be studied separately outside of any reciprocal compromise. Even Euclidian geometry does not represent a purely spatial construct, since we cannot, for example, tackle the demonstration of the Pythagorean theorem without *first* knowing the cases of equality among triangles which, themselves, have as *prerequisite* the knowledge of other developments in geometry reaching, from theorem to theorem, back to fundamental postulates. Whether fast or slow, here there is a movement of the mind through time, or through representation of the past by memory, and occasionally, distant times. Even the Pythagoreans who proceeded through elementary geometry, we are told, more by dint of visual evidence than by reasoning, could not dispense with recalling certain axioms as anterior conditions requisite to trigger judgment or the sense of truth attributed to a conclusion that is always, however slightly, posterior to the premises.

Logic is a Function of Time

The necessity for a temporal order does not represent a particular characteristic of geometric reasoning: it partakes in all logical series. Hence in any syllogism such as, "Negroes are black, Tom is a negro, thus Tom is black," the major and minor premises must necessarily precede the conclusion to make it valid through an effect of causality: it is because Tom belongs to the negro race that he is black. Certainly, this relation of causality is not defined only by the temporal order in which propositions are presented.[23] Nonetheless, this order is a *sine qua non* of this causality. Similarly, in the relations, "Peter is better than John and John is better than Paul," leading to the conclusion that "Peter is better than Paul," we observe an irreversible series, that is, a temporal function. Indeed, from the fact that Peter is better than Paul and John better than Paul, we cannot conclude that Peter is better than John.

Hence, the fourth dimension, at the same time that it orients from the past to the present and the present to the future, the whole continuum in which thought moves, confers a causal meaning to that frame, impressing a unidirectional vectorial progress upon rationalization. Space, in becoming space-time, is also endowed with logical polarization.

Nor is There any Time without Space

A musical melody has sometimes been offered as an example of a mono-dimensional construct within pure duration.[24] Yet a causal chain manifests itself within it, as is clear to the judgment of whoever has some notion of the laws of harmony. Even in abstracting these laws, is it possible that a creative thought or the memory of a melody could develop, albeit implicitly, without using any part of the spatial framework in which this melody is to appear or did appear in the guise of a sensible reality? This seems doubtful, even impossible. We thus cannot absolutely affirm that causality belongs exclusively to the lone dimension of time, although we must at the very least recognize that the causal relation is directly and narrowly subjected to the play of temporal perspective.

The Antilogic of Reverse Time

As noted earlier, the anomalies of causality correspond to particular states of the temporal dimension. And this relation determines, at least partially, the indetermination of certain phenomena, since our mind is shaped in such a way that it must also seek the cause of an absence of cause. This is because the induction of cause to effect and effect to cause constitutes one of the primordial movements of thought and intervenes in almost all the operations of intelligence, which does not seem to know how to function without putting it into motion: it is practically impossible to conceive of a logical series which would not contain, patently or latently, a relation of causality, that is, a necessary order of succession—a time-value.

Since it is a function of time, which is a variable, logic itself is therefore a variable. Hence in the instantaneous present or in eternity, for time-values that are null or infinite, time distances become moot and no order of succession, no logical series, may be established. At that point, reasoning vanishes in the coalescence or dispersal of its terms among which premises and conclusions can no longer be discerned, whether they are punctually fused or, on the contrary, forever separated as if independent of each other.

For finite but reverse time-values, on the other side of zero, logic reappears as definite but also inverted—a logic against sense, an antilogic, as it were, by comparison with the succession of normal time, but not illogical as it is in the absence of succession characterizing the instantaneous and the eternal. The cinematograph is the only apparatus that presents us with a complete and rigorously exact visual aspect of this antilogic that is just as determined as logic, but which is nothing more than the mirror-image on the other side of the dead center of time. At the sight of such a retrograde universe, perhaps we do not discover, though we certainly understand less poorly, that the space of our thought assumes a fifth dimension, or better yet a fifth direction: that of logic, whose variations are directly proportional to those of a temporal dimension within the reciprocal covariance and the general relativity of the space-time-causality continuum.

The Law of Laws

There Is Only Inner Truth

Any philosophy is a system closed upon itself, and the truths contained within it are merely interior. Platonism is true for whoever thinks like Plato; Rousseauism for whoever is moved the way the Solitary Walker was moved; Pragmatism for whoever believes what William James believed. The difficulty begins—insurmountably so—when we presume to judge who is truer, Malebranche or Spinoza, Leibniz or Schopenhauer, for we would need a criterion outside the compared systems, a common measure borrowed from reality. But such reality always eludes inquiry and we must renounce uncovering it and recognize it as unknowable.

What right have we to ask of the cinematographic robot-philosopher to provide more than human philosophers can? The latter deliver an ingenious and somewhat coherent representation of the universe, open to the play of interpretation of appearances on the condition of remaining true to its organic laws; a representation devoid of too many internal contradictions, or at the very least, allowing for subterfuges capable of conciliating them. In the context of this limited ambition, the cinematograph presents, better than any human thinker could, a guarantee of self-coherence, regardless of its inability to escape from mechanical sequencing, to which its mechanical nature ties it, more strenuously than how the human organism is subject to human logic.

A Universe with Variable Time

In its very innate and inescapable construction, the cinematograph represents the universe as an always and everywhere mobile continuity, much more continuous, fluid, and agile than our directly sensible continuity. Heraclitus had not imagined such an instability in all things, such an inconstancy of categories flowing one into the other, such a flight of matter running, ungraspable, from form to form. Rest blossoms into movement and movement fructifies into rest; certainty is alternatively the mother and the daughter of chance; life comes and goes though substances, disappears and reappears, becoming vegetal where we thought it mineral, or animal where we believed it vegetal and human; nothing separates matter and spirit that are like the liquid and the vapor of the same water whose critical temperature would have an absolute lack of constancy; a deep unison circulates between origin and finality and cause and effect as they exchange roles, substantially indifferent to their function. Like the philosopher's stone, the cinematograph holds the power of universal transmutations. Yet, this secret is extraordinarily simple: all its magic devolves from its capacity to vary temporal dimensions and orientations. The truest, most astounding, and perhaps most dangerous glory of the Lumière brothers is not to have spun the development of a "seventh art," especially since it seems to have currently abandoned its true way and is satisfied with being an ersatz of theater. No, its glory is having created a form of witchcraft akin to that of the prophet Joshua, which frees our worldview from servitude to the single rhythm of external, solar and terrestrial time.

Time: The Plasma-Maker [*plasmateur*] of the World

A time variation is enough to cause the unknown that we call reality to become continuous or discontinuous, inert or alive, brute matter or flesh endowed with instinct or an intelligent soul, determined or random, subject to logic or a contrary logic, or a logic that would not fit into any reasonable order. All the primordial semblances of everything that can or cannot be perceived, and all that exists or does not, communicate among themselves, more than likely transform into each other according to particular laws, but also and above all according to an absolutely general law of correlation with the values that the time variable can adopt. The unspeakable reality that we assume to be subjacent to all these qualities created by a temporal perspective is eager to clothe them according to whatever time dimension we lend to this reality.

This law, the great revelation of the cinematographic transcription of the universe, is established in this system with all of the rigor we might require of the most certain of scientific laws. Not only does this supreme law govern all others, either directly or by orienting in one way or another the major components that dictate the transformations of entropy-energy and gravitation, but it also authorizes or prohibits the very conception of a causal or statistical law, and even more generally, the idea of any relation of succession.

A General Law Governs a General Substance

Out of this dominant law of all the architectural formulas of creation there results a confirmation and a new aspect of absolute monism, which alchemy had predicted and science rediscovers at its slower pace. Under its illusory diversity, nature is incapable of displaying any essential difference to us since attributes are only labile and one is convertible into the others *ad libidum temporis*. Without these differences, some necessity must exist for the uniformity of the unknown that alternatively supports this or that quality. "All things spring from a unique thing," asserts the Emerald Table, and we cannot ask more of this text, both too admired and too ridiculed, overrated either way, which claims to summarize the millenary gnosis of alchemy and the Kabbalah—themselves the heirs of more ancient forms of esoteric thought—into twenty lines of a text stuffed with elemental and astrological allegories whose key is now lost.[25]

Indeed, whether we call it God or the Quintessence of Energy, the unique essence of all things divided into appearances remains unapproachable. It is not entirely impossible to hope that one day we will spend our vacations on an astro-port of Venus or Mars, that we will manufacture armies of homunculi, that truth and lies will be electroscoped, that we will buy tubes of fluorescent thoughts and pill bottles full of the toxins of love and courage, leniency, and friendship. But even if the universe may be stripped of all its other mysteries, it will more than likely, through the quiddity of its nature and down to the last analysis of its substance, always keep asking a question that has no answer. This is not an unresolved problem: we feel that it is insoluble. It amounts to a notion that dwindles, disintegrates, and vanishes into understanding the more the latter tries clearing it up. Among so many hunts for the ungraspable, that of Descartes is perhaps the defeat in which the inanity of a chimera transpires the most clearly, escaping through the sieve of thought which we realize contains, at last, nothing that may be expressed. All we can guess of this nothing is that it is everywhere the same: this is because, depending on its movement in space-time, it sustains all appearances indifferently.

The Mystery of Simplicity

Summarizing an unfathomable tradition, the Kabbalah and alchemy posited, and nearly claimed to, demonstrate the substantial and functional unity of the universe. The microcosm and the macrocosm were held to fundamentally possess the same nature and to both obey the same law. Generally speaking, the current development of science is on a path to confirming this prodigious intuition. The cinematograph also brings an experimental confirmation to it. It intimates that the substance of all sensible reality, notwithstanding our inability to conceive of what it is, behaves everywhere and at all times as if, truly, it was everywhere and at all times identical to itself. The cinematograph also shows that this singular unknown is governed, in all its differentiations, by a first law: the attribute is a function of time, the variations of quality follow the variations of time quantity, or better yet, of space-time quantity, since time is in fact inseparable from the space it orients.

Hence in the structure of nature as a whole, through infinitely entangled details, thought observes or creates a perfectly general axis, a directing avenue, or a path toward comprehension that is surprisingly straight. Confronting such a simplification, our first reflex is to protest, as if we'd seen through the complicated gestures an illusionist employs to hide the secrets of his tricks: "That's all it was!" Yet, upon further reflection, this simplification itself constitutes a new enigma, another deeper and perhaps inaccessible mystery. It seems that, stripped of the embellishments of illusion, we suddenly discover the incomprehensible: true magic.

Irrealism

The Cinematographic Schema of the Universe

The little we know of extreme reality and ultimate objects is, first, that they are everywhere equal to themselves, identical by nature; second, that they are located in a four-dimensional space-time continuum with a causal or logical polarization; and third, that the movement of these real elements of an unqualifiable but single nature, within a four-coordinate reference system, is enough to create the innumerable variety of all phenomena. Such is the schema of the cinematographic representation of the universe reduced to its simplest expression.

Movement:
The Condition of Reality

Yet time, as we have seen, does not exist in itself: it is but a perspective produced by the succession of events, that is, by the relation of their positions relative to the fourth vectorial axis of the reference system. Time is the effect of a particular mobility of the elements of reality as they transit from past to future. Without this mobility there would be no time, and objects could not aspire to a temporal reality.

But space does not possess any proper existence either: it too is merely a relation, albeit of coexistence, between phenomena; it is merely a perspective, albeit of simultaneity; the consequence of extensions or displacements measured relatively to the other three axes of the system. Gauged by sight, hearing, touch, even smell, these displacements give form to the imaginary space, and absent these displacements, we would be incapable of having the slightest idea. If immobile, objects could possess neither spatial nor temporal reality.

Like space and time, the causality of space-time is merely a pure ghost as well, a tendentious interpretation of space-time relations of succession and coexistence. Without the movement of objects, which produces these relations, no semblance of determination would therefore be possible.

Hence, the indivisible atom of reality retains a certain complexity: first, it contains being, which, however named, we haven't succeeded in conceiving as insubstantial; second, it comprises the location of being in space and time; third, as we've just explained, it includes the movement of being. Without movement, nothing can be real. Reality presents itself as a synthesis of substance and movement from which results its requisite space-time location and, potentially, its apparent determinism.

The Pluralism of Reality

Nonetheless, if reality consisted of a single mobile element, that is to say, if it was a moving continuum, could it create the causal space-time continuum in which we locate it? Apparently not. For a single element that is always identical to itself can neither form relations of co-existence nor succession, nor cause and effect relations: it thus could engender neither space, nor time, nor causality. Such an element cannot be located: being everywhere at all times, it is nowhere and never, because, if we cannot define where it is not, we can no better determine where it is. Thus it can claim no right to spatial or temporal reality. Hence, the unique element that would only possess the bare property of being could not really exist.

From this, we understand that being, as pure substance, has no more reality than space, time and cause. First or last, the elementary substance we call matter or energy, alone in itself, amounts to a flagrant unreality.

Reality Exceeds Substance

Since reality cannot be conceived as an elementary continuity, we must suppose that it is a collection of grains of reality. Indeed, in such discontinuity, relations of co-existence and succession can appear and install time and space. And it is from such reciprocal relations among elements that fundamental substance, mobile and granular (whatever it may be), receives the right of space-time existence, with a quadruple location and a logical orientation, without which there is no reality. The latter can thus not be considered inherent to any substance. A substance that is not mobile and multiple, albeit equal to itself, remains unreal since it cannot be located. Reality, inscribed in space-time, is essentially bound up with time and space relations.

Substance Does Not Contain Reality

As for the reality of substance that we might take to be the thing in itself par excellence, it is not even what we might viably call an idea. Posited in its pure and simple state, substance derives from the category of false concepts in which all we can grasp is what it does not contain. It is an excessive abstraction, the schematization of such a multitude of particular cases, which in the end corresponds to none of them and nothing at all. This root—to the Nth power—of sensible reality is but a very vague imagination, a mad myth, and could only return to figure something actual if it lent itself to a space-time location.

The Metaphysics of Realism

If the mind cannot succeed in accepting the reality of an object that cannot be located, if a thing that is nowhere cannot be thought, conversely, it is less difficult to imagine a location without being preoccupied with the necessity of its hypostasis. Problems such as those dealing with the encounter of two punctual mobiles, that is, materially unreal, are already familiar to young school children. Probably, even the purest form of mathematics cannot succeed in completely severing itself from the idea of substance as support. Still, we must recognize that there are degrees of reality, as for all complex notions, and that relations of space-time seem sufficient, almost in themselves, for creating a kind of reality, albeit unsubtle.

In any case, within the mixture that constitutes the everyday notion of reality, it is its space-time location or relation that plays the most important part. Yet, in itself, it is nothing like a substance: clearly it is metaphysical and impresses this characteristic upon any conception of reality. This is even more so the case today to such an extent that we recognize that no precise location can be established without a certain probability. At bottom then, reality can never be a certainty, only a supposition. And this hypothetical aspect, as outlined by Heisenberg's inequalities, does not seem to be a temporary accident, due to a rectifiable deficiency of experimental instrumentation, but it is an essential trait, necessarily inherent to the most advanced mathematics of realism.

Substance is an Artifice of Thought

Let us conclude that in the universe, as represented by the cinematograph, space-time relations constitute the essential factor of a reality whose substance only exists through the faculty of being localized, however uncertainly, in space-time. The only discernible essence in an object is then its value of space-time position relative to other objects, none of which possesses a more concrete or stable nature. The ultimate thingness, since it is merely a set of complex relations or a function of variables, is necessarily a variable itself. It is a metaphysical phenomenon produced by the confluence of several perspectives and it also amounts to an effect of perspective, albeit multiple perspectives: the greater the number of axes of representation at play, the stronger the reality effect [*effet de réalité*] that will be obtained.[26]

Hence, at first, a one-dimensional figure, a line without any thickness, can hardly be conceived of as real. But the two-dimensional figures of plane geometry already derive an impression of reality that captivates school children from this first dimensional multiplicity. It is only upon painstaking reflection that they accept the fact that the circles and polygons they ponder really only have an ideal nature, and through their harmonies produce nothing more than a transcendental truth, a mathematical poetry. Then the convergence of the three spatial dimensions confers a much greater degree of veracity to spheres and polyhedrons, and the superior realism these lines inspire translates into the label of "solid" that we give them. Nonetheless, everyone must admit that in spite of themselves, geometry in space is no less virtual than on a plane, it is quite the opposite: if a simple line is unreal, what are a square and a cube if not the imaginary to the second and third power respectively? Ultimately, the perspective of phenomena thickens with a fourth dimension in the domain of mechanics, that of movements in time. The object acquires an opacity that has the color of reality and thereby almost perfectly conceals its true constitution: a coalescence of four species of unreality, a fourth power of the imaginary.

Hence, a sufficient multiplication of falsity tends to produce truth by itself. We stumble again, in its clearest example, on the law by which quantity engenders quality: the imaginary, combined fourfold to the imaginary, becomes real. Yet on the display case of this reality, it would be more honest to add the label: FACTITIOUS.

Even Essence is nothing but an Attribute

The antiphilosophy of the cinematograph thus holds reality to be fundamentally unreal, that is, unsubstantial: all substance amounts to a sum of sufficiently large imaginary data. We could call this system unrealism, although it does not deny the function of reality, but considers it to be a secondary phenomenon resulting from the multiplication of axes of reference, in relation to which this semblance may be located. A representation inscribed on a plane determined by two coordinates can only claim a very weak reality, while a figure defined according to the five kinds of possible relations in causal space-time is, by this very fact, charged with the maximum reality-quality that we are able to recognize in an image. In the end, reality does not exist as an essence: it is but an attribute that accompanies a certain degree of complexity, thickness, and density of thought laboring to formulate a more or less restricted zone of the space-time continuum.

The Inhuman Share in a Robot's Philosophy

Of course such a philosophy cannot claim to be perfect, and it cannot develop without the difficulties from which we extricate it, so as to send it on its way, only with the help of barely disguised analogies. The main issue is that the cinematograph, albeit while flinching, occasionally leaps from the subjective to the objective, and vice versa: the thinking machine, like a primitive consciousness, hardly distinguishes one from the other. This is a grave deficiency according to the rules of classical systems.

However, this essay endeavored to discern, as sharply as possible, the particular way in which the cinematograph suggests a worldview that is also particular. If I had not respected the detours and shortcuts of the very special consequences of cinematographic pre-thought, I could have sketched a less shocking system, easier and better suited to human norms, but further from the originality of the model.

Today, computing machines calculate somewhat more correctly, but still in the very same style as humans: they were devised precisely for this activity, by imitating the process of human arithmetic. By contrast, the inventors of the cinematograph—who were numerous—never had the ambition of constructing a philosophizing machine in order to rethink the attributes and categories, the relations of space and time, or statistical and causal series, in the way humans do. The cinematograph was at first a mere recording gaze interested in all the world's spectacles. Then it was employed for the analysis of quick movements and for the discovery of slow movements. At the same time or later on, we taught it to enlarge the infinitely small, to make the infinitely far closer, and ultimately, after numerous attempts, we added an ear to this eye as well as an organ of elocution. And suddenly we realized that we had in fact created a kind of partial mechanical brain registering visual and auditory stimuli, which it coordinates in its own way in space and time, and which it expresses in the elaborate form of often astounding combinations, out of which a plentiful philosophy is emerging that is just as astounding. Philosophy is, to be sure, neither entirely random nor completely foreign to the human intelligence from which it was indirectly born: yet it is the philosophy of a robot-brain that was neither intentionally nor strictly programmed to accomplish a work identical to that of the living organ.

A Philosophy is a Local Phenomenon

That the philosophy of the cinematograph may not be viable outside of the screen, that it may perhaps not carry over to the world in which we ordinarily live, cannot constitute an indictment against it. The architecture of any ideological edifice can only be validly judged according to the specifications given to the architect, that is to say, only according to the constraining data and limits through which the construction was made. Euclidian geometry proves inapplicable to the whole of the universe, though it remains supremely exact within the perimeter of the city of Paris. Determinism falters inside the atom, but it continues to insure a hefty certainty with respect to the forecasting of innumerable events of daily life. We might think that many systems who maintain opposing truths would destroy each other, while in fact they coexist in peace, either by ignoring each other or harmoniously overlapping, since each system only governs its own domain.

Lack and Necessity of Pain

Ultimately, there is a very general objection that may be addressed to any ideology wherein the birth and development of a mechanical apparatus plays as important a role as it does in the present case which we are dealing with here, which is unique in the history of thought.

Such a philosophy appears to rest on rather shaky grounds, insofar as it makes use of mechanically produced data, because although we can praise their objective value, to some extent these always lack a subjective value which is much more—if not exclusively—necessary and sufficient to give credit to a theory. The regard given to objectivity is indeed greatly exaggerated. Besides the fact that it would be inconceivable, a perfectly objective science or philosophy, would neither interest, nor convince, nor serve anyone, because it would have no human meaning. What we routinely call objectivity is merely an average degree of subjectivity through which almost all humanity can communicate and understand each other. So long as the working of a machine does not move our sensibility and thereby participate in our inner life, it is of no help to our thinking or to our belief in what we think. Therefore, a mechanism must first be endowed with a *sui generis* sensibility that may be joined [*raccorder*] to ours.[27]

Yet in the case of cinema there is not only a particular and multiple sensibility, but also a varied capacity to combine and transform the data of this sensibility from which results a kind of psychic activity and subjective life that prepare and thereby orient the intellectual work of humans.

However, when intelligence operates on the direct data of human sensibility, its authenticity is perfectly ascertained, in the last analysis, by a control which, although also subjective, is unimpeachable: that of pain. Thought has only ever convinced a few thinkers (if any!) that they really existed—but pain, which makes the utmost use of sensibility, allows no one to doubt that they're suffering, thus that they exist.

In that regard, the data from mechanical sensibility cannot secure in itself this supreme confirmation of the undeniable subjective state that pain causes. To be sure, a machine grates and grinds, heats up, strains, weakens, or falters, thus displaying symptoms corresponding to minor indispositions, the vague precursors of organic pain. It is not only, nor precisely, through a metaphor that one speaks of the diseases from which metals and rocks "suffer." *Sunt lacrymae rerum.*[28] But these tears shed by things remain too obscure and are known only through mediation. They remain too distant from us to be able to confer this absolute degree of certainty upon a mechanical sensibility, which humans find within themselves as evidence of their subjective experiences. From here we get the renunciation and the inability of any mechanical philosophy, especially that of the cinematograph, to affirm and know the reality of substance. No being can encounter the latter but in its own passion for life. The mechanized philosophy of the cinematograph lacks this ability, from itself and without intermediary, to be confirmed by the indispensable necessity of pain that produces the only indisputable objectivity in an absolutely subjective form.

Return to Pythagorean and Platonic Poetry

In summary, the spectacle of the universe animated on screen invites us to conceive of a reality whose nature differs considerably from the one figuring in most classical philosophies. It is a reality that does not rely on substance and that acknowledges its almost purely metaphysical character. It consists chiefly in a mode of location within space-time, the result of the grouping of the four space-time relations establishing a relationship between one point and another. The physicist André-Marie Ampère distinguished three sorts of reality: phenomenal, noumenal, and relational. These relations devolve from mathematical and mechanical functions that are, in this case, implemented by a machine. Whether we think of them mechanically or organically, relations remain ideas, ideas about numbers. Reality amounts to ideas and numbers.

It is not so much that humans or their machines discover a reality that would preexist, but rather one that they construct according to the pre-established mathematical and mechanical rules of space-time. Reality, the only knowable reality, does not exist: it is manufactured, or more precisely, it must be manufactured. This is only possible through the pre-conceived framework determined by the constitution of the operator that activates the formula, that is, through the thinking apparatus, whether it be human or inhuman. This is true everywhere. The experimentation that proceeds from an ideological plane creates experimental results from which we cannot infer anything concerning the nature of reality that would have pre-existed them, free of any observation. An experiment is never impartial: at its most honest it is tendentious, it only proves that which it was built to prove, in the same way that an apple tree, structured to make apples, could never make coffee beans.

The cinematograph is also an experimental apparatus that constructs, that is to say, thinks an image of the universe whose reality is predetermined by the structure of its plasmatic mechanism.[29] In the same manner that a thermometer, an eye, a clock, an ear, or an electroscope can only know or isolate, that is, invent realities that are respectively thermal, luminous, gravitational, sonorous, or electrical; or again that an altimeter or a chronometer are able to choose, that is, to imagine, among all the possibilities of reality, only spatial and temporal values; moreover the cinematograph merely possesses the mandatory faculty to realize—to render real—the combination of space and time, providing the product of space and time variables, which means that cinematographic reality is therefore essentially the idea of a complete mode of location. Yet it is only an idea, an artificial idea, of which we can only affirm an ideological and artificial existence—a kind of trick or special effect. Nonetheless, this trick is extremely close to the process by which the human mind itself conjures up an ideal reality for itself.

It is likely that the idea, the very first idea, that which is not quite yet an idea, emerges from the contact and authority of sensible reality (sensible for humans or machines). But this seed of thought subsequently detaches itself from reality, the way a seed leaves a tree, developing into a true idea by itself which, in turn, recreates reality in its image and usage in order to govern it. Auguste Comte asserted that "the mind is not meant to rule but to serve." Still, for the mind to be useful and to serve, it must first rule.

In this manner, the cinematograph brings us back to Pythagorean and Platonic poetry: reality is but the harmony of Ideas and Numbers. In truth, science, even unbeknownst to itself, has never stopped conforming its progress to this conception that dates back two millennia. But today, the primacy of the mathematical poem is no longer a secret. Physics willfully admits that it can only know, has only ever known, and will forever know reality under the guise of the possible, that is to say, in the form of numerical rules prescribing the conditions under which reality is ultimately allowed to produce itself. Extreme reality no longer exists as a place of substance, but as a set of algebraic formulas. These formulas outline or, more properly speaking, create a specific and fictive zone in space that is the locus of this extreme reality - and no one knows how to get any closer to it.

Translator's Endnotes

1. By "vitalists" Epstein does not mean followers of Bergson or Whitehead, as we do today, but Gnostics and Kabbalists for whom the word encompasses living *personae* (hence the "personalism").

2. The pair *pondérable/impondérable* plays an important role in Epstein's thought: it comes from Lat. *pondere*, which means "to weigh," and figuratively "to think," and thus directly links materiality and thought (the word "essay," as in Montaigne's *Les Essais*, also carries the sense of materiality assayed via the intellect).

3. The word *cristallin* means both a budding crystal and the lens of the eye: the importance for Epstein of scientific films of crystal growth becomes clearer with this double meaning.

4. The word "coenesthesis" (distinct from synesthesia) is now replaced in psychology by the expression "enteroceptive sensations," that is, the feelings we have of the inside of our own bodies (whether muscular, skeletal, gastro-enteric, respiratory, cardiac, urinary, sexual, thermal, etc.). For Epstein, cinema represents a unique apparatus allowing us to perceive enteroception differently, and he places it at the core of his theory of both poetry and *photogénie*.

5. The expression "*pellicule de chagrin*" is untranslatable: it refers to novelist Honoré de Balzac's novel *La Peau de chagrin* (1831), a title translated both as *The Wild Ass Skin* and *The Magic Skin*, in which a protagonist finds a magic skin from a wild ass (called shagreen, a word of Turkish origin) that grants him any wish, yet shrinks every time he uses it. The word "pellicule" means literally "very thin skin," and refers in common French to film-stock or film–strip.

6. This refers to a corpus of hermetic writings from the Middle-Ages and the Renaissance, which attributed the origin of alchemy and other occult sciences to Hermes Trismegistus (thrice-great).

7. "Eaux-mères" is a rare expression in French, likely playing off the homonyms *mer/mère* (sea/mother) and not unrelated to the 'oceanic feeling' of Otto Rank. Epstein uses it in *a Poésie d'aujourd'hui, un nouvel état d'intelligence. Paris: La Sirène, 1921* to describe coenesthesis (see note 4).

8. Astronomer Urbain Le Verrier (1811-1877) hypothesized on the basis of orbital anomalies the existence of a planet beyond Jupiter: Neptune was indeed discovered using his calculations in 1846.

9. This phenomenon is known as the redshift in cosmology, or the Doppler-Fizeau effect in astronomy: since all stars display this shift toward the red in their wavelength, it suggests that the universe is expanding.

10. Contemporary psychology has confirmed this trend. See Daniel Wegner, *The Illusion of Conscious Will* (New York: Bradford Books, 2003).

11. This radical view conforms with the "absolute contingency" of all laws of the universe recently propounded by a philosopher belonging to speculative realism, Quentin Meillassoux, *After Finitude: An essay on the Necessity of Contingency*, trans. Ray Brassier, (London: Bloomsbury, 2010).

12. The psychologist Théodule-Armand Ribot (1839-1916) who strongly influenced Jean-Paul Sartre among others.

13. Epstein is punning on the title of Bergson's first book, *Time and Free Will: An Essay of the Immediate Data of Consciousness* (*Les Données immédiates de la conscience*).

14. Philosopher and priest Nicolas Malebranche (1638-1715) was a follower of Descartes known for developing the theory of occasionalism placing God in charge of all efficient causes.

15. Lucretius, *De Natura Rerum*, LIV, iv. "D'en plus parler je me desiste / Tout n'est qu'*abusion* (I desist from saying more / All is but abuse), François Villon (1431-1464), Ballade des seigneurs du temps jadis. Voltaire (1694-1778), *Observations du commentateur sur Judith*.

16. We should keep in mind that Epstein was a gay man forced to be closeted who did advocate for a broader notion of "normalcy."

17. Epstein's speculations are here again ahead of their time: facial analysis software offers the troubling promise of deep psychological surveillance.

18. Epstein reverses here his initial condemnation of psychoanalysis expounded in "Freud, or the Nick-Carterianism in Psychology" (1921).

19. This is another convergence with Gilles Deleuze's thought, namely his notion of "the body-without-organs" in *A Thousand Plateaus* trans. Brian Massumi (Minneapolis: University of Minnesota Press, 1987).

20. The emphasis of Gilles Deleuze on the brain in the second volume of his two books on cinema, *The Time-Image*, is clearly beholden to Epstein. He cites Epstein's collected works (36 n.15) and refers directly to *The Mind of the Apparatus* (181). Gilles Deleuze, *Cinema 2: The Time-Image*, trans. Hugh Tomlinson and Robert Galeta (Minneapolis: University of Minnesota Press, 1989).

21. This is another major dig at Bergson whose central philosophical tenet puts quality over quantity, and separates them absolutely.

22 In the "Categories" and "Topics" sections of *The Logic*, Aristotle defines ten logical categories: the second and third are quality and quantity.

23. The last sentence seems to draw attention to the issue of the relativity—Epstein's master word in this book—of race construction undergirding the syllogism. Let's recall that a few pages earlier Epstein declared that snow has no inherent color, and could well "be black," which is then a pure secondary attribute. Anthropologist Jean Rouch said that he brought only one book with him to Africa—Epstein's *L'intelligence d'une machine*—precisely because it deconstructs a good deal of the scaffoldings of certainty on which France's racist colonization was more or less implicitly built.

24. Bergson's *Matter and Memory* was among the first to do so (New York: Zone Books, 19.

25. *The Emerald Tablet*, attributed to Hermes Trismegistus, was based on an Arabic text of the 6ᵗʰ to 8ᵗʰ century titled *Kitāb sirr al-halīqa* (*Book of the Secret of Creation and the Art of Nature*) written by a Neo-Pythagorean philosopher, the Pseudo-Appolonius of Tyana (from Cappadocia, in today's Turkey). It was translated into Latin in the 13ᵗʰ century and Isaac Newton, a lifelong alchemist, penned a translation into English.

26. Epstein's "effet de réalité" may have left its mark of Roland Barthes' "effet de réel." In the late 1950s Barthes was associated with the Institut de Filmologie where Epstein gave courses in the early 1950s. Roland Barthes, "L'Effet de réel," *Communications* 11 (1968), 84-89.

27. Epstein makes often use of terms of art of the film industry that he translates into quasi-concepts: the words '*superposer*' and '*superposition*', which meant "superimposition" or "composite shot" are one example. Here "*raccorder,*" which means "to join' or 'to couple,' conceals the meanings of 'splicing' the film strip as well as "shot transition."

28. "Sunt lacrimae rerum et mentem mortalia tangut," translates as "there are tears of/for things and mortal things touch the mind." It is a quote from Book I, line 462 of the *Aeneid* of Virgil.

29. Epstein uses the word "*dispositif*" for "apparatus" in a way that combines here the materiality of technology with what he calls its ideology, or power of representation. Michel Foucault would later develop a very similar concept for the same word "*dispositif*" as a confluence of material and ideological effects. We don't know whether Foucault read Epstein, so the striking convergence of their thoughts might be coincidental or not.

Univocal Publishing
123 North 3rd Street, #202
Minneapolis, MN 55401
www.univocalpublishing.com

ISBN 9781937561185
This work was composed in Berkley Oldstyle.
All materials were printed and bound
in February 2014 at Univocal's atelier
in Minneapolis, USA.

The paper is Mohawk Via, Pure White Linen.
The letterpress cover was printed
on Crane's Lettra Fluorescent.
Both are archival quality and acid-free.